CALIFORNIA American His

Growth and Conflict

myWorld INTERACTIVE

Active Journal

Savvas Learning Company LLC, 15 East Midland Avenue, Paramus, NJ 07652

Cover: Tetra Images/Getty Images

Attributions of third party content appear on page 246, which constitutes an extension of this copyright page.

ISBN-13: 978-0-32-896020-0
ISBN-10: 0-32-896020-9
15 21

CONTENTS

Review Topic
Connecting with Past Learnings

Topic 1
The Revolutionary Era (1750–1783)

Topic 2
A Constitution for the United States (1776–Present)

Topic 3
The Early Republic (1789–1825)

Topic 4
The Age of Jackson and Westward Expansion
(1824–1860)

Topic 5
Society and Culture Before the Civil War (1820–1860)

Topic 6
Sectionalism and Civil War (1820–1865)

Topic 7
The Reconstruction Era (1865–1877)

Topic 8
Industrial and Economic Growth (1865–1914)

Topic 9
The Progressive Era (1865–1920)

REVIEW TOPIC

Connecting with Past Learnings Preview

Essential Question Why do people move?

Before you begin this topic, think about the Essential Question by answering the following questions.

1. List some reasons why people might leave their homes and settle elsewhere.

2. Preview the topic by skimming lesson titles, headings, and graphics. Then place a check mark next to the names of the people you predict will play an important role in the early European settling of the Americas.

__Olaudah Equiano	__Christopher Columbus	__John Locke
__George Whitefield	__Henry the Navigator	__Galileo Galilei
__Marie Curie	__Mary Todd Lincoln	__George Washington

Timeline Skills

As you read, write and/or draw at least three events from the topic. Draw a line from each event to its correct position on the timeline.

1200	1300	1400

Map Skills

Using maps throughout the topic, label the outline map with the places listed. Then color in the New England Colonies, the Middle Colonies, and the Southern Colonies, using a different color for each category. Create a map key to tell what each color represents.

Rhode Island	Connecticut	New Hampshire	Massachusetts
Delaware	New York	New Jersey	Pennsylvania
Maryland	Virginia	Georgia	North Carolina
South Carolina			

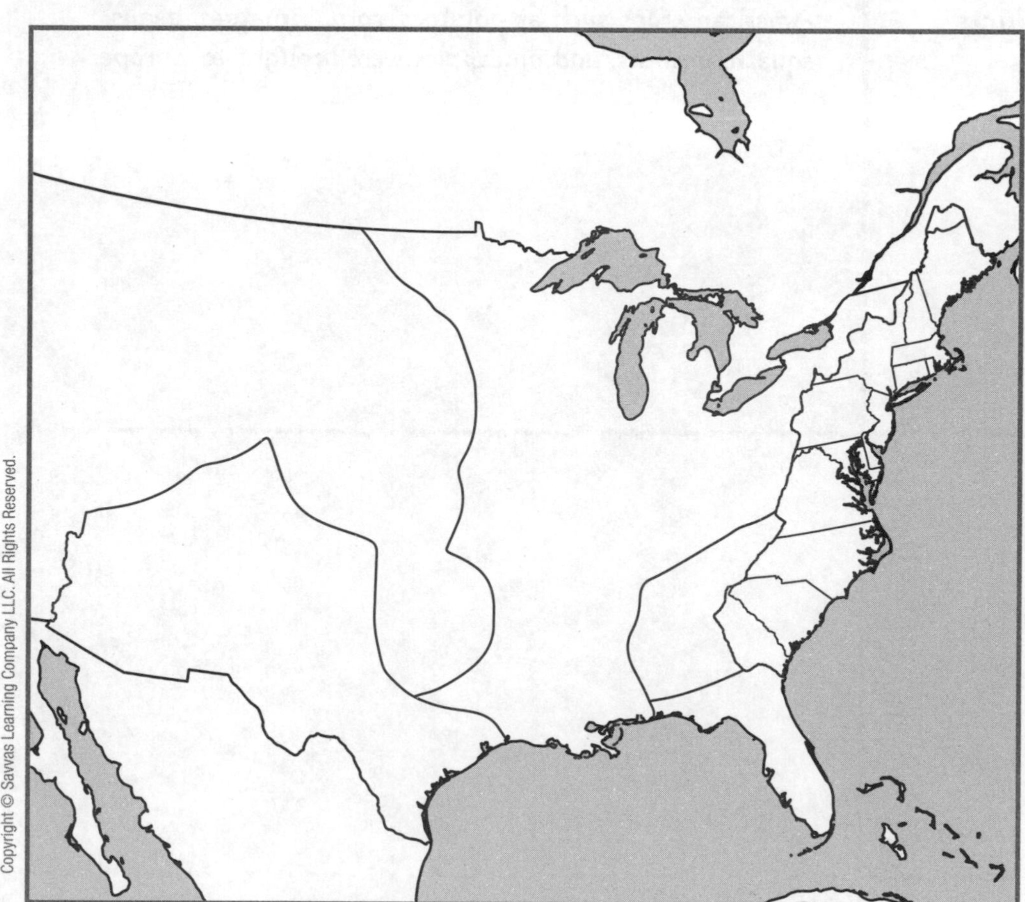

1500 | 1600 | 1700 | 1800

Take Notes

Literacy Skills: Identify Cause and Effect Use what you have read to complete the table. In each space, write one effect of the Columbian Exchange. The first one has been started for you.

What was exchanged?	Effect of Columbian Exchange
New Products and Ideas	• American crops such as potatoes, corn, tomatoes, beans, squash, peanuts, and pineapples were brought to Europe.
Disease	
Slavery	

INTERACTIVE

For extra help, review the 21st Century Tutorial: **Analyze Cause and Effect**.

Practice Vocabulary

Words in Context For each question below, write an answer that shows your understanding of the boldfaced key term.

1. How did **cartographers** assist in the exploration of the globe?

2. What is a **plantation**, and who was brought to plantations?

3. In what time frame did the **Renaissance** take place, and what kinds of new discoveries were made during the period?

4. What is a **colony**, and who governs it?

Take Notes

Literacy Skills: Summarize Use what you have read to complete the chart. In each column, write four details that support the main idea. Then write a summary statement about what Europeans aimed to accomplish with these colonies. One detail has been completed for you.

Jamestown Colony Details	Plymouth Colony Details
A group of investors received a charter.	

Summary:

INTERACTIVE

For extra help, review the 21st Century Tutorial: **Summarize.**

Practice Vocabulary

Vocabulary Quiz Show Some quiz shows ask a question and expect the contestant to give the answer. In other shows, the contestant is given an answer and must supply the question. If the blank is in the Question column, write the question that would result in the answer in the Answer column. If the question is supplied, write the answer.

Question	Answer
1.	1. capitalism
2.	2. northwest passage
3. What is the name for a political system in which voters elect others to make laws?	3.
4. What kind of official document gives certain rights to an individual or group?	4.
5.	5. mercantilism
6.	6. religious freedom
7. What is a percentage that a lender adds to the original amount?	7.

Take Notes

Literacy Skills: Compare and Contrast Use what you have read to complete the Venn diagram. List characteristics of the New England Colonies and Southern Colonies in the correct area of the diagram. The first one has been completed for you.

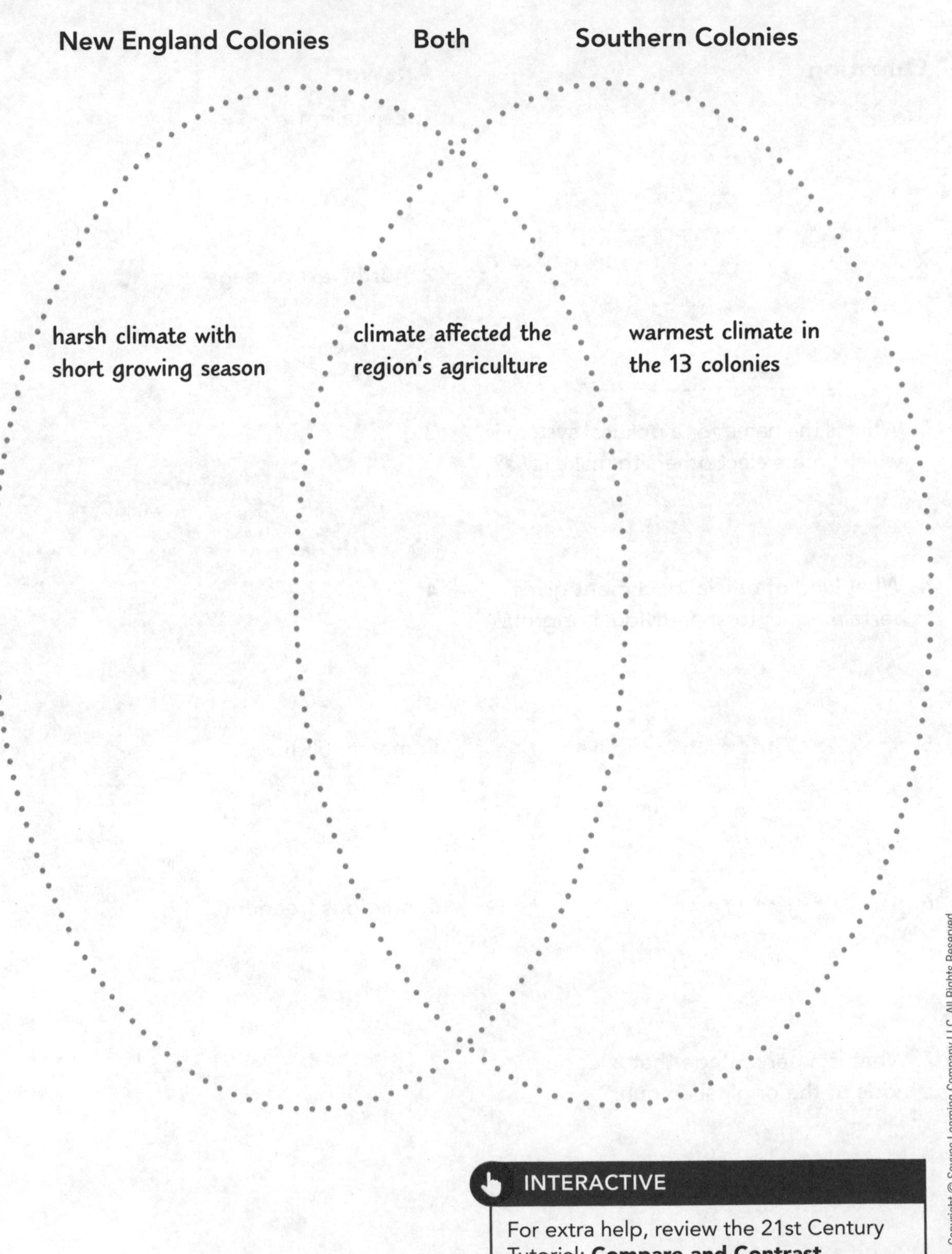

INTERACTIVE

For extra help, review the 21st Century Tutorial: **Compare and Contrast**.

Practice Vocabulary

Sentence Revision Revise each sentence so that the underlined vocabulary word is used logically. Be sure not to change the vocabulary word. The first one is done for you.

1. Cash crops are used by the farmer who grows them.
   Cash crops are sold by the farmer who grows them.

2. William Penn was a Quaker, a member of a small Protestant sect that taught that some people have more rights than others.

3. In the New England colonies, families did subsistence farming, selling what they produced.

4. A debtor is a person who takes something, such as money, from someone else.

Take Notes

Literacy Skills: Identify Main Ideas and Details Use what you have read to complete the charts. Identify main ideas related to the subject and provide supporting details. One has been completed for you.

Enlightenment's Major Influences and Applications	
Great Awakening	• new kinds of churches arose, forcing religious tolerance • encouraged a spirit of independence • if people could worship on their own, they could govern themselves
Scientific Revolution	
Politics	

Enlightened Thinkers Who Influenced Colonists	
Sir Isaac Newton	
John Locke	
Charles-Louis Baron de Montesquieu	

INTERACTIVE

For extra help, review the 21st Century Tutorial: **Identify Main Ideas and Details**.

Practice Vocabulary

Sentence Builder Finish the sentences below with a key term from this section. You may have to change the form of the words to complete the sentences.

Word Bank

enlighten	libel	separation of powers
divine right	reason	natural right

1. Thinkers freed from the ignorance of the Middle Ages were called

2. When an individual thinks in a logical way, he or she is using

3. Absolute monarchs claimed that God gave them authority to rule, a belief known as

4. A person who publishes statements that damage another person's reputation can be charged with

5. Life, liberty, and property are

6. Division of power between government branches is called

Writing Workshop Arguments

As you read, build a response to this question: **How did the moral and political ideas of the Great Awakening affect the development of revolutionary fervor and morality?** The prompts below will help walk you through the process.

Lesson 1 Writing Task: Consider Your Purpose and Audience

(See Student Text, page 13)

Write a sentence that expresses your opinion on the topic and addresses your readers. This will be your claim for the argument you will write at the end of the topic.

Lessons 2 and 3 Writing Task: Support Claims

(See Student Text, pages 20 and 25)

As you read these lessons, gather evidence to support your claim. Your evidence must support your claim.

Evidence
•
•
•

Lesson 4 Writing Task: Write an Introduction

(See Student Text, page 35)

Write a paragraph introducing your claim about the Great Awakening and your evidence. Your introductory paragraph should be clear and concise.

Writing Task Using the claims and evidence you gathered, answer the following question in a five-paragraph argument: How did the moral and political ideas of the Great Awakening affect the development of revolutionary fervor and morality?

As you write, consider using the following words and phrases to transition between points: *because*, *since*, *in addition*, *consequently*, *therefore*, and *of course*.

The Revolutionary Era Preview

Essential Question When is war justified?

Before you begin this topic, think about the Essential Question by answering the following questions.

1. What are good reasons for going to war? Put a check mark next to the reasons that you think would prompt a justifiable war.

__ Too many taxes

__ No voice in government

__ Government cuts off trade with the world

__ Government punishes illegal acts of civil disobedience

__ Government keeps soldiers among the people in times of peace

__ Government forces people to house soldiers

__ Government officers inspect the cargoes of ships for no reason

2. Look at the items you checked. Is any one, by itself, a good enough reason to go to war? Or would it take more than one of these reasons to justify a war?

Timeline Skills

As you read, write and/or draw at least three events from the topic. Draw a line from each event to its correct position on the timeline.

1750	1760	1770

Map Skills

Using maps throughout the topic, label the outline map with the places listed. Then color in the territory claimed by Britain and Spain.

New Hampshire	Massachusetts	New York	Connecticut
Rhode Island	New Jersey	Pennsylvania	Delaware
Maryland	Virginia	North Carolina	South Carolina
Georgia			

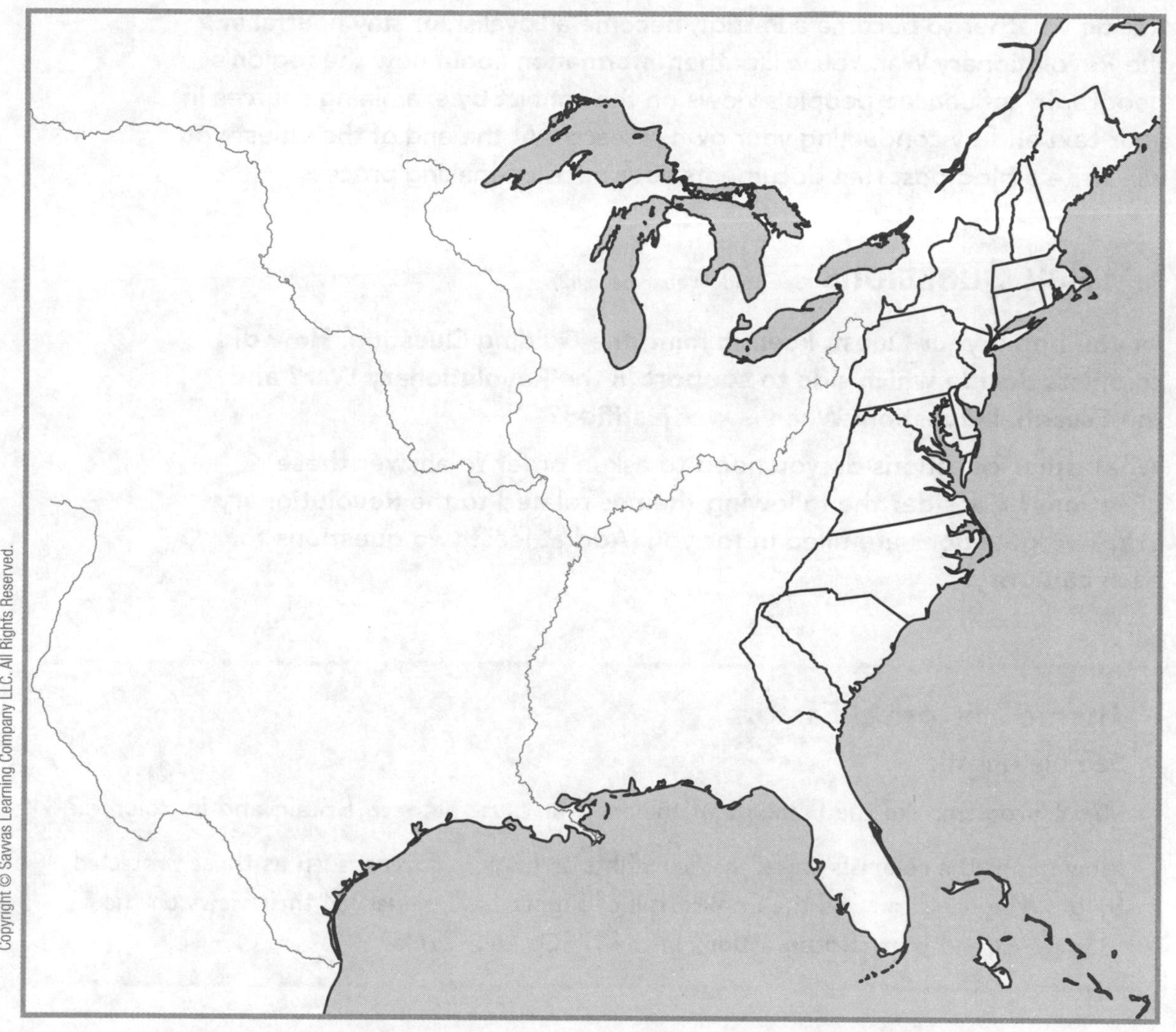

1780 1790

Choosing Sides

On this Quest, you are living in the Chesapeake Bay region in 1776 and must decide whether to become a Patriot, become a Loyalist, or stay neutral in the Revolutionary War. You will gather information about how the region's geography influenced people's views on the conflict by examining sources in your text and by conducting your own research. At the end of the Quest you will write a blog post that documents your decision-making process.

1 Ask Questions (See Student Text, page 42)

As you begin your Quest, keep in mind the Guiding Question: **How did colonists decide which side to support in the Revolutionary War?** and the Essential Question: **When is war justified?**

What other questions do you need to ask in order to answer these questions? Consider the following themes related to the Revolutionary Era. Two questions are filled in for you. Add at least two questions for each category.

Theme Historical Factors

Sample questions:

What problems did the French and Indian War cause between Britain and its colonies?

How might the colonists' belief in their rights as English citizens, such as those protected by the Magna Carta and the English Bill of Rights, have influenced their views on the Stamp Act and other British actions in the 1760s and 1770s?

Theme Society and Demographics

Theme Geography and Economy

Theme Land and the Proclamation of 1763

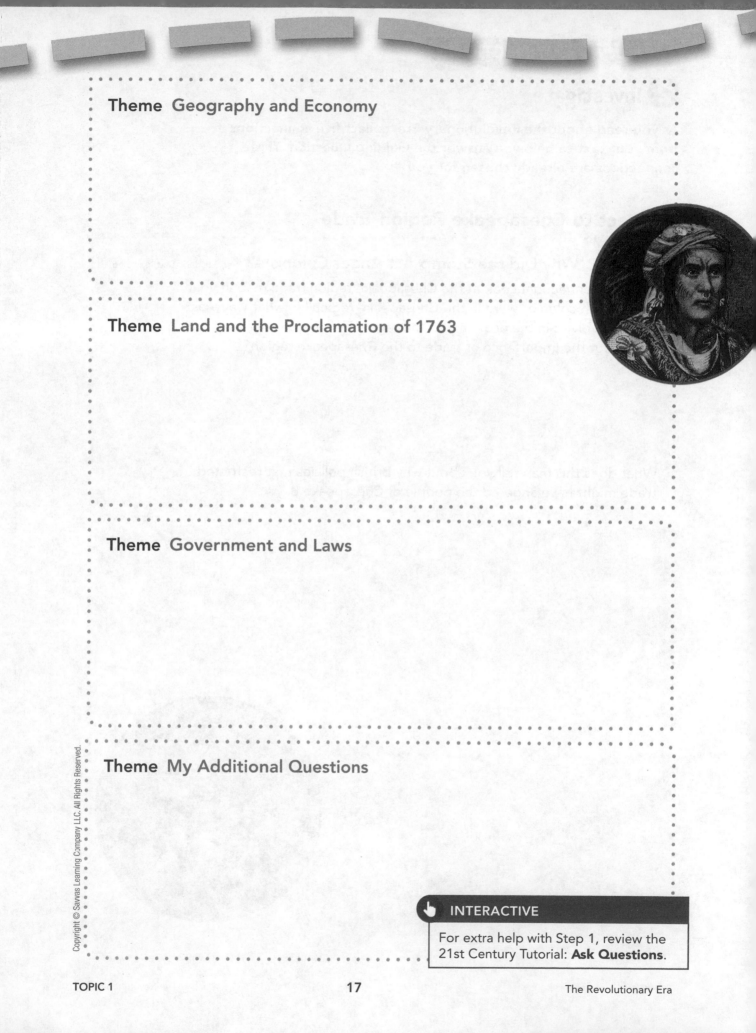

Theme Government and Laws

Theme My Additional Questions

INTERACTIVE

For extra help with Step 1, review the 21st Century Tutorial: **Ask Questions**.

2 Investigate

As you read about the Revolutionary Era, collect five connections from your text to help you answer the Guiding Question. Three connections are already chosen for you.

Connect to Chesapeake Region Trade

Lesson 2 Why Did the Stamp Act Anger Colonists? (See Student Text, page 56)

Here's a connection! Look at the Chesapeake region trade map in your text. Which colonies were in the Chesapeake region? In what way was Britain involved in the economy of the region? What does this map tell you about the importance of trade to the Chesapeake region?

What does this map tell you about why British policies that restricted trade might have angered the people of Chesapeake Bay?

Connect to Thomas Paine's Ideas

Lesson 4 What Did Thomas Paine Say in *Common Sense*?

(See Student Text, page 77)

Here's another connection! Thomas Paine was a British-born writer who lived in Philadelphia and tried to encourage colonists to resist the British government and King George III. What does the excerpt from his writing say about the importance of kings compared to ordinary, honest men?

How do you think colonists might have reacted to this argument?

Connect to *Common Sense*

Primary Source Thomas Paine, *Common Sense*

(See Student Text, page 87)

What arguments does this connection offer to those who were deciding whether to support the Patriots or Britain? Thomas Paine's pamphlet was distributed throughout the colonies. Was he a Patriot or a Loyalist? What does Paine have to say to those who felt an obligation to the king?

According to the essay, why did Britain offer help and protection to the colonies?

It's Your Turn! Find two more connections. Fill in the title of your connections, then answer the questions. Connections may be images, primary sources, maps, or text.

Your Choice | Connect to

Location in text

What is the main idea of this connection?

What does it tell you about how the colonists decided which side to support during the Revolutionary War?

Your Choice | Connect to

Location in text

What is the main idea of this connection?

What does it tell you about how the colonists decided which side to support during the Revolutionary War?

3 Conduct Research (See Student Text, page 100)

Form teams based on your teacher's instructions. Meet to decide who will create each segment of your blog. In the chart below, record which team member will perform which task. You will research further only the segment that you are responsible for. Use the ideas in the connections to further explore the subject you have been assigned. Pick who or what you will write about, and find more sources about that subject. Be sure to find valid sources, and take good notes so you can properly cite your sources. Record key information about your area of research here.

Team Member	Segment	Specific Topic of Segment
	Historical Factors	
	Society and Demographics	
	Geography and Economy	

INTERACTIVE

For extra help with Step 3, review the 21st Century Tutorials: **Work in Teams, Search for Information on the Internet,** and **Avoid Plagiarism.**

4 Create Your Blog (See Student Text, page 100)

Now it's time to put together all the information you have gathered and use it to write your segment of the blog.

1. **Prepare to Write** You have collected connections and explored primary and secondary sources that tell you about the Chesapeake Bay region during colonial times. Look through your notes and decide which facts would help you decide whether to be a Patriot, Loyalist, or neutral colonist. Record them here.

2. **Write a Draft** Decide as a team which side of the war you will support. Then write a draft of your segment of the blog, explaining how your assigned theme affected your team's decision. Include any maps or images that might help illustrate your position. Be sure to include evidence that you have gathered and citations for the evidence used.

3. **Share with a Partner** Once you have finished your draft, ask one of your team members to read your draft and provide comments on the clarity and flow of the information. Revise the segment based on his or her comments, and comment on his or her segment, if possible.

4. **Put Together Your Blog** Once all team members have written and revised their segments, it's time to put them together. As a team, discuss how you will organize your information. Be sure to write smooth transitions from one segment to the next and finish with a strong conclusion.

5. **Present Your Blog** Present your completed blog to your classmates as a group. Listen to the other teams' blogs, and take notes on the information they shared using a separate sheet of paper.

6. **Reflect on the Quest** After all the presentations, discuss your thoughts on your blog and the other blogs. Reflect on the project and list what you might do differently next time so the teamwork goes more smoothly.

Reflections

INTERACTIVE

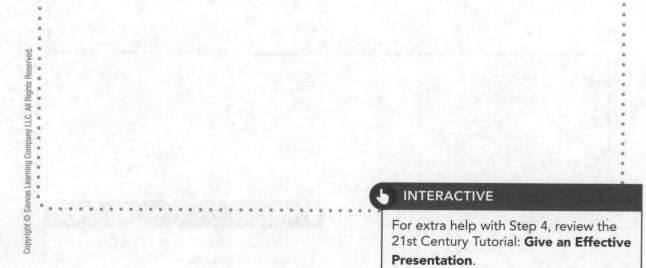

For extra help with Step 4, review the 21st Century Tutorial: **Give an Effective Presentation**.

Take Notes

Literacy Skills: Sequence Use what you have read to complete the flow charts. Each box contains a specific event, and the boxes are placed in the order in which events happened. The first one has been completed for you.

George Washington and the French and Indian War

- Washington works as a land surveyor.

The French and Indian War from 1757 to 1763

INTERACTIVE

For extra help, review the 21st Century Tutorial: **Sequence**.

Practice Vocabulary

Word Map **Study the word map for the term *French and Indian War*. Characteristics are words or phrases that relate to the word or words in the center of the word map. Non-characteristics are words and phrases not associated with the word or words. Use the blank word map to explore the meaning of the term *Treaty of Paris*. Then make word maps of your own for these terms: *ally* and *Albany Plan of Union*.**

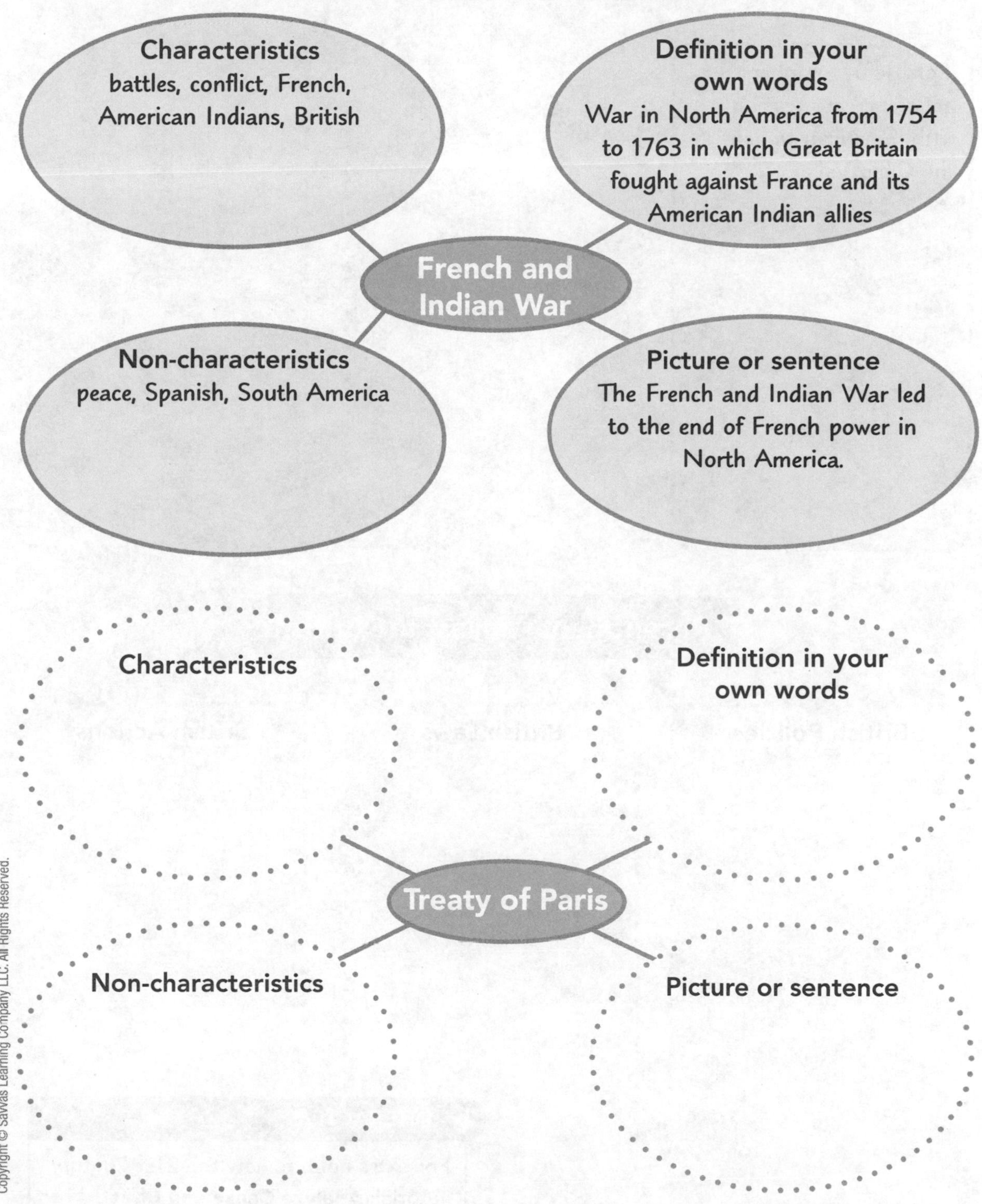
Characteristics
battles, conflict, French, American Indians, British
Definition in your own words
War in North America from 1754 to 1763 in which Great Britain fought against France and its American Indian allies
French and Indian War
Non-characteristics
peace, Spanish, South America
Picture or sentence
The French and Indian War led to the end of French power in North America.
Characteristics
Definition in your own words
Treaty of Paris
Non-characteristics
Picture or sentence

Take Notes

Literacy Skills: Identify Cause and Effect Use what you have read to complete the charts. The top box contains the effect and the boxes below contain the causes. The first one has been completed for you.

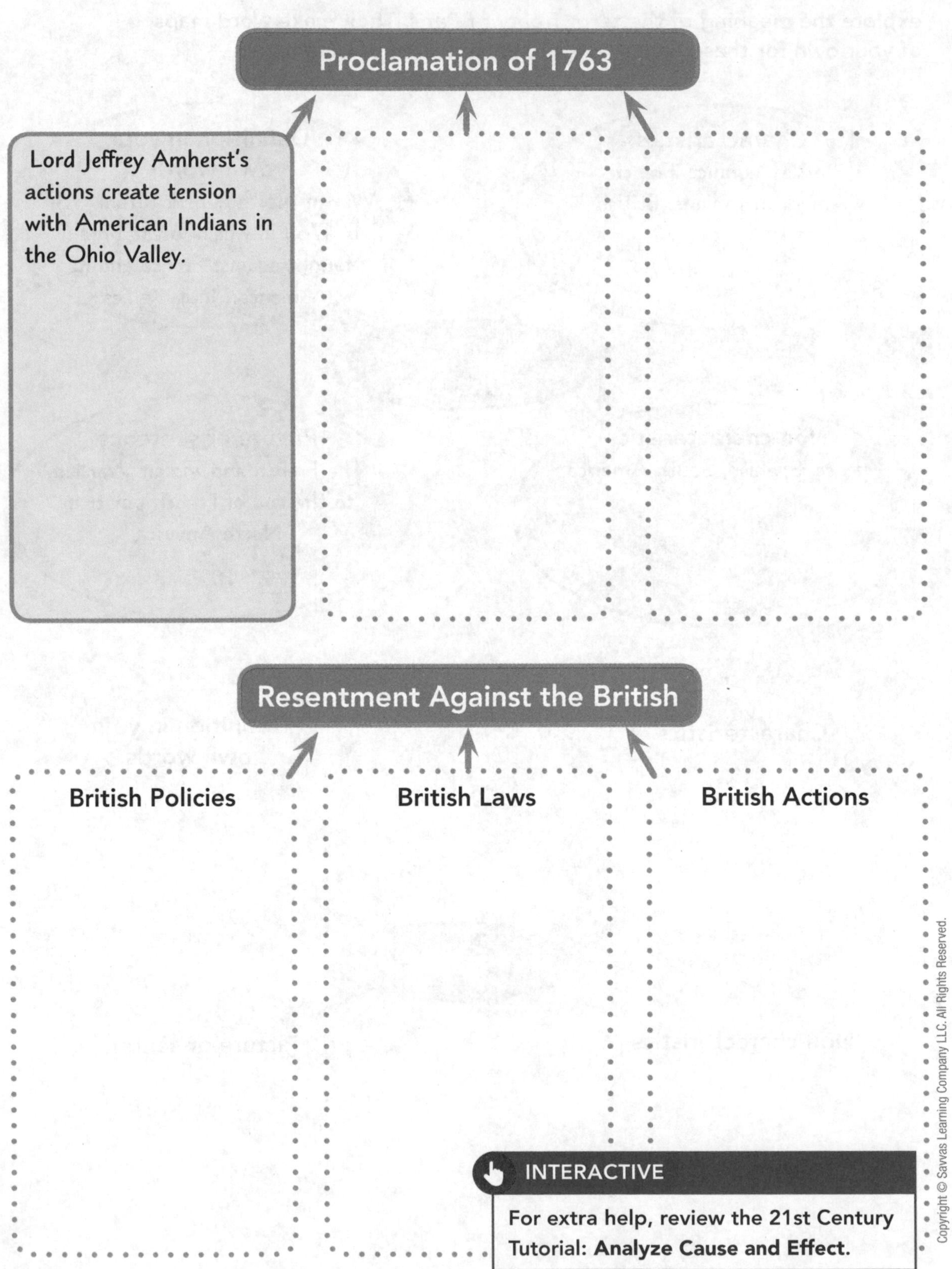

INTERACTIVE

For extra help, review the 21st Century Tutorial: **Analyze Cause and Effect.**

Practice Vocabulary

Sentence Builder Finish the sentences below with a vocabulary term from this section. You may have to change the form of the words to complete the sentences.

Word Bank

petition	boycott	repeal
writ of assistance	committee of correspondence	

1. A formal written request signed by a group of people is called a

2. Parliament cancelled the Stamp Act, which means that the act was

3. Legal documents that allowed British customs officers to inspect a ship's cargo without giving a reason were called

4. When the colonists refused to buy British tea, they were

the tea.

5. Colonists who joined letter-writing campaigns to protest British policies were members of a

Quick Activity Make a Timeline

With a partner or small group, examine this painting of George Washington during the Battle of Monongahela during the French and Indian War.

Did you know?

During the war, George Washington learned that American Indian battle tactics were very effective against British troops.

What does this portrayal of George Washington tell you about how he was viewed? How did the French and Indian War lead to conflicts and actions that contributed to the start of the American Revolution?

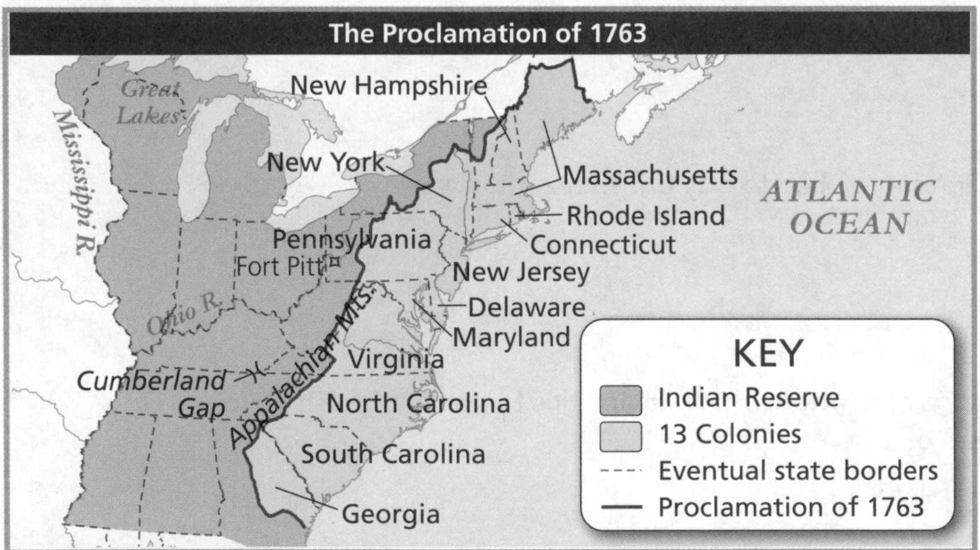

Team Challenge! How does this map relate to the causes of the American Revolution? Create a timeline of major events and ideas that led to the American Revolution, such as the ones depicted in these images. Add events and ideas as you read and explain the significance of each. Add some images to help illustrate your timeline.

Take Notes

Literacy Skills: Summarize Summarize the content of the main headings in this lesson using the tables on this page. As you work, pay special attention to the subheadings in the reading. The first main idea has been completed for you.

The Boston Tea Party	How Did King George III Strike Back at Boston?	The Battles of Lexington and Concord
Main Idea: Colonists protest the Tea Act.	**Main Idea:**	**Main Idea:**
Details: Parliament kept the tax on tea when it repealed all other taxes with the Townsend Act. The Tea Act of 1773 cut out American merchants from the tea trade. Americans boycotted tea and drank coffee.	**Details:**	**Details:**

The Fighting Continues	Opposing Sides at War
Main Idea:	**Main Idea:**
Details:	**Details:**

INTERACTIVE

For extra help, review the 21st Century Tutorial: **Summarize**.

Practice Vocabulary

Vocabulary Quiz Show **Some quiz shows ask a question and expect the contestant to give the answer. In other shows, the contestant is given an answer and must supply the question. If the blank is in the Question column, write the question that would result in the answer in the Answer column. If the question is supplied, write the answer.**

Question	Answer
1. What is the name for colonial volunteers who were ready to fight at any time?	1.
2.	2. Loyalists
3.	3. civil disobedience
4.	4. Patriots
5. What is the term for an army of citizens who serve as soldiers during an emergency?	5.

Take Notes

Literacy Skills: Use Evidence Use what you have read to complete the concept webs. Enter evidence in the outer circles that supports the main idea in the center circle. The first circle has been filled in for you.

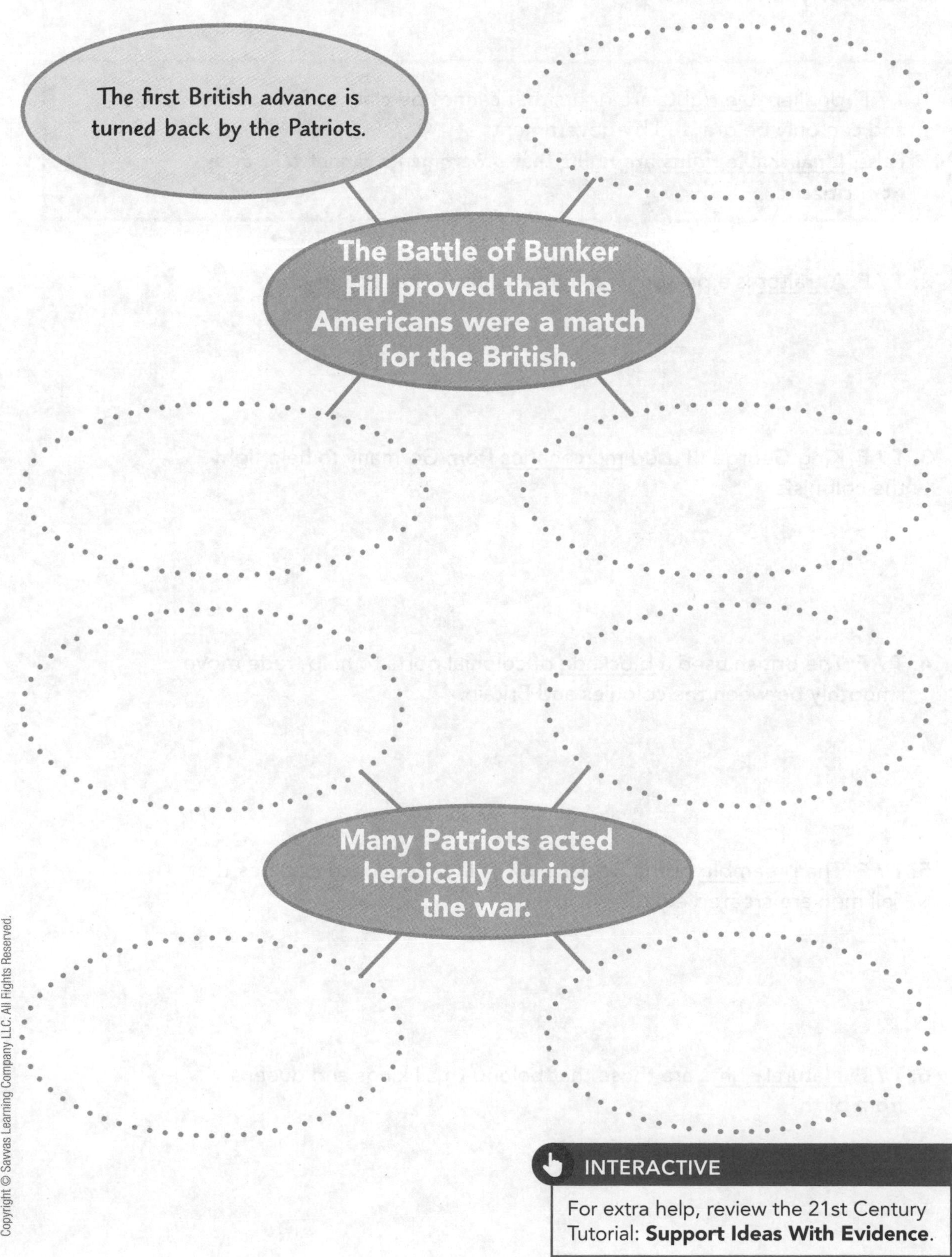

The first British advance is turned back by the Patriots.
The Battle of Bunker Hill proved that the Americans were a match for the British.
Many Patriots acted heroically during the war.

INTERACTIVE

For extra help, review the 21st Century Tutorial: **Support Ideas With Evidence**.

Practice Vocabulary

True or False? Decide whether each statement below is true or false. Circle T or F, and then explain your answer. Be sure to include the underlined vocabulary word or words in your explanation. The first one is done for you.

1. **T / F** Unalienable rights are rights that cannot be claimed by citizens and can only be granted by governments.
   False; Unalienable rights are rights that governments cannot take away from citizens.

2. **T / F** A traitor is a person who fights for his or her country.

3. **T / F** King George III used mercenaries from Germany to help fight the colonists.

4. **T / F** The British used a blockade of colonial ports to help trade move smoothly between the colonies and Britain.

5. **T / F** The preamble of the Declaration of Independence declares that "all men are created equal."

6. **T / F** Natural rights are those that belong to all kings and queens from birth.

Quick Activity Edit the Declaration

Thomas Jefferson wrote the first draft of the Declaration of Independence in June 1776. Afterward, he made some revisions to the document himself, and Benjamin Franklin and John Adams also made some changes. When the Declaration was presented to the Second Continental Congress, still other changes were made.

Here is the original version of Thomas Jefferson's Preamble to the Declaration.

Did you know?

After the 1941 bombing of Pearl Harbor, the Declaration was placed in a padlocked bronze container, guarded by Secret Service agents, and temporarily moved from the National Archives to Fort Knox.

> We hold these truths to be sacred & undeniable; that all men are created equal & independent, that from that equal creation they derive rights inherent & inalienable, among which are the preservation of life, & liberty, & the pursuit of happiness. . . .

Working in pairs, one partner should write the original version of the Preamble on a piece of paper. The other should write any phrases from the final version of the Preamble (below) that differ from this original version on sticky notes. For example, you will have one sticky note that reads *self-evident*. Also use blank sticky notes to "cross out" words. Work together to use your sticky notes to change the original Preamble until it reads as the final version does.

> We hold these Truths to be self-evident, that all Men are created equal, that they are endowed by their Creator with certain unalienable Rights, that among these are Life, Liberty, and the Pursuit of Happiness.

Team Challenge! Work with your partner to answer this question: Why were these changes made to the Preamble? Give a possible reason for each change that was made.

Take Notes

Literacy Skills: Sequence Use what you have read to complete the timeline. Look for key events that fall within the dates on the timeline as you read. Add those events to the timeline by entering the event in one of the spaces provided and then connecting the event to the appropriate place on the timeline. The first one has been completed for you.

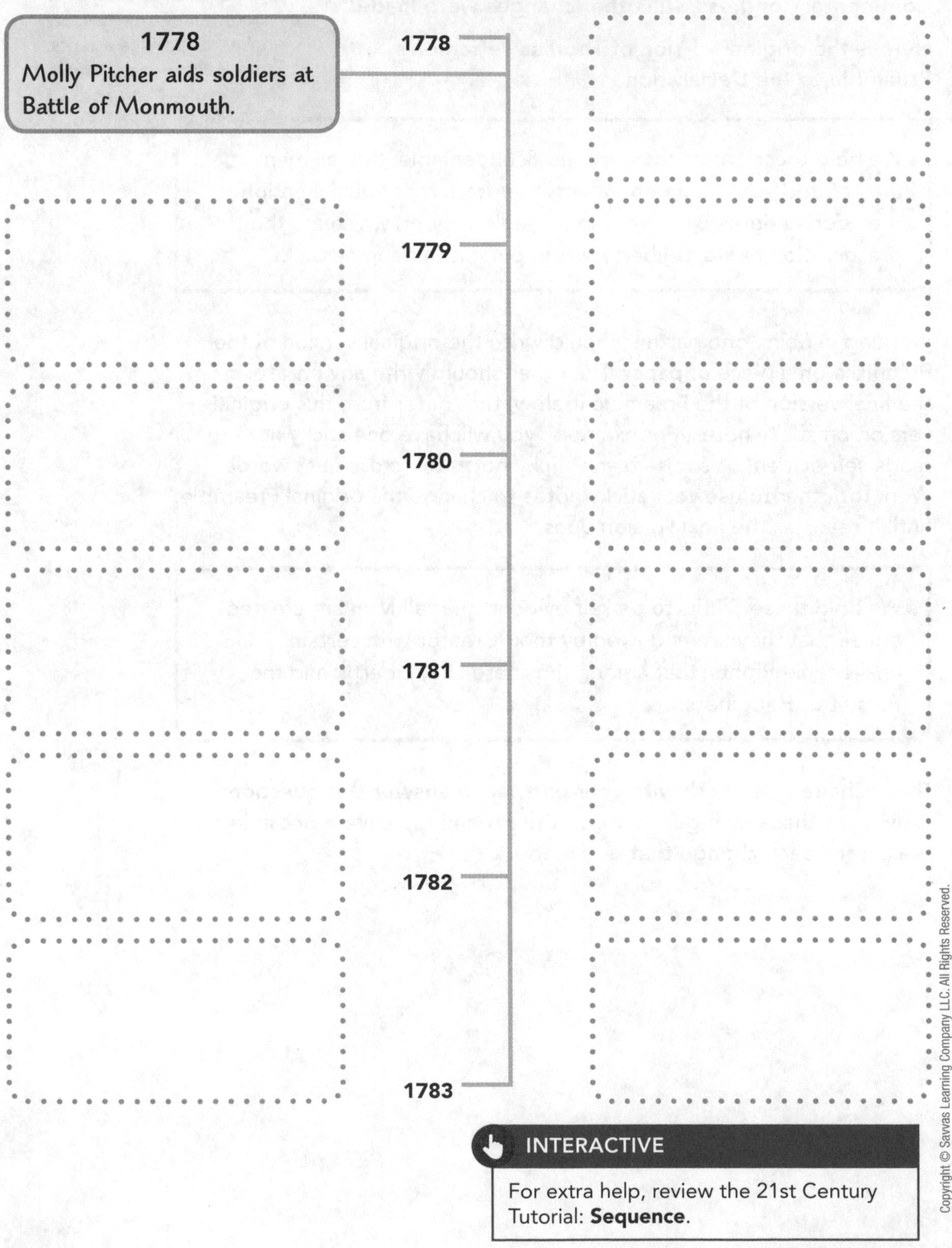

INTERACTIVE

For extra help, review the 21st Century Tutorial: **Sequence**.

Practice Vocabulary

Matching Logic **Using your knowledge of the underlined vocabulary words, draw a line from each sentence in Column 1 to match it with the sentence in Column 2 to which it logically belongs.**

Column 1	Column 2
1. More than 16,000 American and French troops laid <u>siege</u> to the general's army of fewer than 8,000.	The troops appeared suddenly out of the swamps, attacked quickly, and retreated swiftly back into the swamps.
2. Congress <u>ratified</u> the Treaty of Paris after eight years of war.	Casimir Pulaski trained troops to fight from horseback.
3. American forces included a <u>cavalry</u>.	Less than three weeks later, the British surrendered.
4. Militia led by the Swamp Fox used <u>guerrilla</u> tactics against the British.	The British recognized the United States as an independent nation.

Writing Workshop Explanatory Essay

As you read, build a response to this question: Why was there an American Revolution? The prompts below will help walk you through the process.

Lesson 1 Writing Task: Consider Your Purpose and Audience

(See Student Text, page 50)

Write a sentence that states the purpose of your essay and identifies your audience.

Lesson 2 Writing Task: Develop a Clear Thesis (See Student Text, page 62)

In one sentence, express the most important reason for why the American Revolution happened. This will be your thesis statement for the explanatory essay you will write at the end of the topic.

Lesson 3 Writing Task: Support Thesis with Details (See Student Text, page 73)

Now add details from lessons 1, 2, and 3 to support your thesis statement.

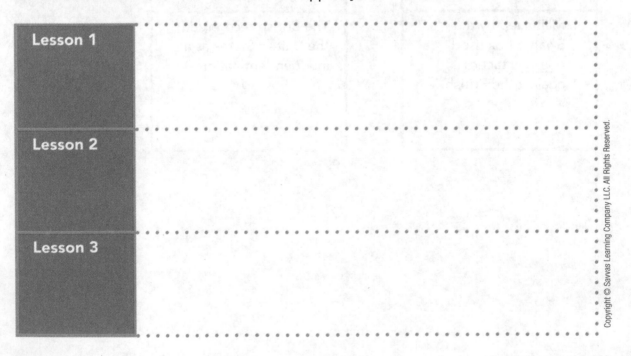

Lesson 1	
Lesson 2	
Lesson 3	

Lesson 4 Writing Task: Pick an Organizing Strategy

(See Student Text, page 86)

Make an outline of your essay. You can organize your essay any way you like. For example, you might focus first on British actions and then on changes in the colonial perspective. Or you might choose to organize by major themes, such as taxes. Use the chart below to decide on a strategy and outline how you will carry it out in each paragraph of your essay.

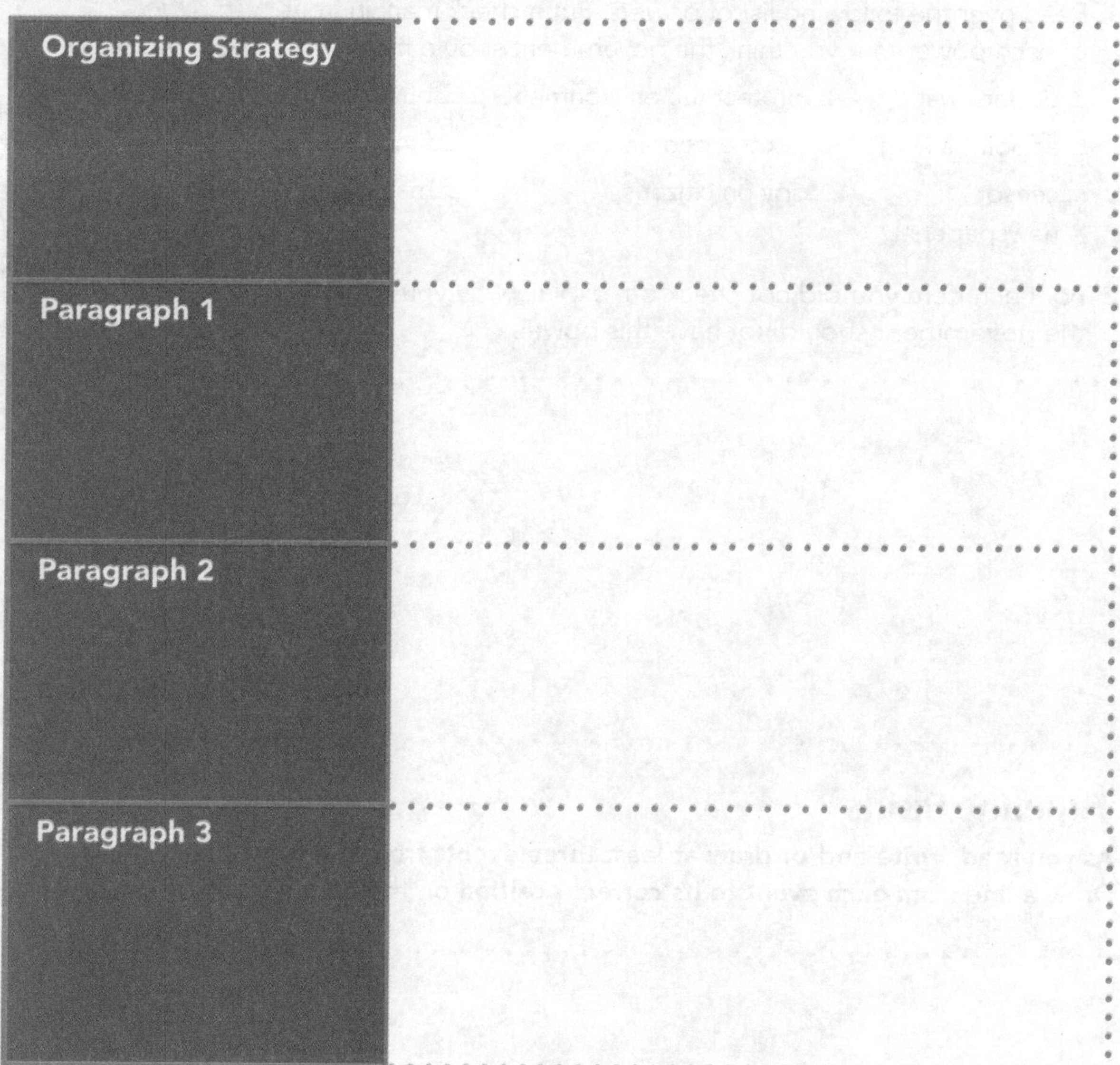

Organizing Strategy	
Paragraph 1	
Paragraph 2	
Paragraph 3	

Lesson 5 Writing Task: Write an Introduction (See Student Text, page 98)

On a separate sheet of paper, write a short paragraph that introduces the thesis of your essay about the American Revolution.

Writing Task (See Student Text, page 101)

Using the outline you created, answer the following question in a three-paragraph explanatory essay: Why was there an American Revolution?

TOPIC 2

A Constitution for the United States Preview

Essential Question How much power should the government have?

Before you begin this topic, think about the Essential Question by answering the following questions.

1. Read over the following list of powers. Put a check mark in front of each power that you think the government should have.

__declare war	__protect the environment	__build roads
__appoint a king	__tax the people	__fund schools
__censor newspapers	__spy on citizens	__make laws

2. For each item you did not check off, explain why you think the government should not have this power.

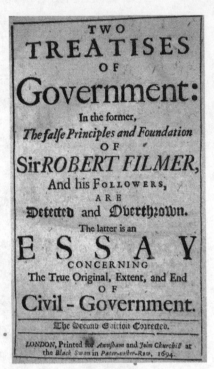

TWO
TREATISES
OF
Government:
In the former,
The false Principles and Foundation
OF
Sir *ROBERT FILMER*,
And his Followers,
ARE
Detected and Overthrown.
The latter is an
ESSAY
CONCERNING
The True Original, Extent, and End
OF
Civil - Government.
The Second Edition Corrected.
LONDON, Printed for *Awnsham* and *John Churchill* at the *Black Swan* in *Pater-noster-Row*, 1694.

Timeline Skills

As you read, write and/or draw at least three events from the topic. Draw a line from each event to its correct position on the timeline.

1770 | 1780 | 1790

Map Skills

Using maps throughout the topic, label the outline map with the places listed. Then shade the disputed western lands one color, Spanish territory a second color, and British territory a third color.

Georgia	Delaware	Connecticut	Virginia
South Carolina	New Jersey	Rhode Island	New York
North Carolina	Pennsylvania	Massachusetts	New Hampshire
Maryland			

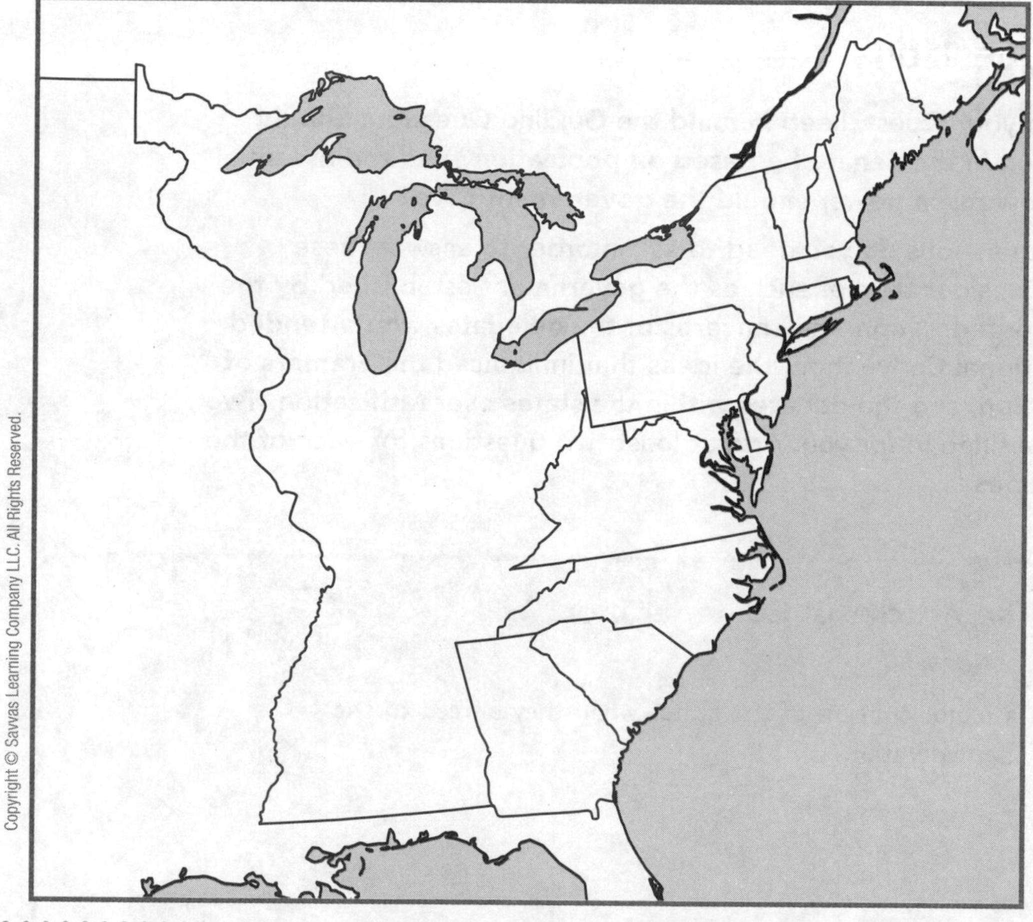

1800 1810

Senate Representation

On this Quest, you will explore sources and gather information about representation in the Senate from the perspective of a U.S. Senator. Then, you will participate in a civic discussion with other legislators about the Guiding Question.

1 Ask Questions (See Student Text, page 106)

As you begin your Quest, keep in mind the Guiding Question: **Should representation in the Senate be based on population?** and the Essential Question: **How much power should the government have?**

What other questions do you need to ask in order to answer these questions? Consider themes such as the government established by the Articles of Confederation, the concerns of the delegates who attended the Constitutional Convention, the ideas that influenced the Framers of the Constitution, and the debates within the states over ratification. Two questions are filled in for you. Add at least two questions for each of the other categories.

Theme The Articles of Confederation

Sample questions:

What was a major concern of the states when they agreed to the Articles of Confederation?

How was representation in Congress determined under the Articles?

Theme **The Constitutional Convention**

Theme **Ideas and Traditions That Influenced the Framers**

Theme **Debates Over Ratification**

Theme **My Additional Questions**

INTERACTIVE

For extra help with Step 1, review the 21st Century Tutorial: **Ask Questions**.

Quest CONNECTIONS

2 Investigate

As you read about the events leading up to and following the drafting of the Constitution, collect five connections from your text to help you answer the Guiding Question. Three connections are already chosen for you.

Connect to Alexander Hamilton

Primary Source Federalist and Antifederalist Writings

(See Student Text, page 133)

Here's a connection! Read the excerpt from Framer Alexander Hamilton. To what criticism of the proposed Constitution is he responding?

According to Hamilton, what is accomplished by equal representation in the Senate?

Connect to The Virginia and New Jersey Plans

Lesson 2 Disagreements Over a New Government (See Student Text, page 116)

Here's another connection! Read the discussion of the Virginia and New Jersey plans in your text. What was the main difference between the two plans?

How did the states respond to these two plans?

Connect to Representation in Congress

Lesson 5 The Legislative Branch—Congress (See Student Text, page 139)

What does this connection tell you about how the number of representatives is decided in each body that makes up the legislative branch? How many representatives does each state get in the House? How many representatives does each state get in the Senate?

Which states have the largest and smallest numbers of representatives?

It's Your Turn! Find two more connections. Fill in the title of your connections, then answer the questions. Connections may be images, primary sources, maps, or text.

Your Choice | Connect to

Location in text

What is the main idea of this connection?

What does it tell you about how representation in the Senate should be determined?

Your Choice | Connect to

Location in text

What is the main idea of this connection?

What does it tell you about how representation in the Senate should be determined?

3 Examine Primary Sources (See Student Text, page 164)

Examine the primary and secondary sources provided online or from your teacher. Fill in the chart to show how these sources provide further information about whether representation in the Senate should be based on population. The first one is completed for you.

Should Representation in the Senate be Based on Population?	
Source	**Yes or No? Why?**
"Democracy-Proof"	YES, *because equal representation unfairly allows a small minority to pass or block laws.*
"Democracy's False Prophet"	
"America the Undemocratic?"	

INTERACTIVE

For extra help with Step 3, review the 21st Century Tutorials: **Compare viewpoints** and **Read Charts, Graphs, and Tables**.

4 Discuss! (See Student Text, page 164)

Now that you have collected clues and explored documents about representation in Congress, you are ready to discuss with your fellow representatives the Guiding Question: Should representation in the Senate be based on population? Follow the steps below, using the spaces provided to prepare for your discussion.

You will work with a partner in a small group of Senators. Try to reach consensus, a situation in which everyone is in agreement, on the question. The people of your state are depending on you!

1. **Prepare Your Arguments** You will be assigned a position on the question, either YES or NO.

   My position:

   Work with your partner to review your Quest notes from the Quest Connections and Quest Sources.

   - If you were assigned YES, agree with your partner on what you think were the strongest arguments from Scialabba.
   - If you were assigned NO, agree on what you think were the strongest arguments from Gordon and Zakaria.

2. **Present Your Position** Those assigned YES will present their arguments and evidence first. As you listen, ask clarifying questions to gain information and understanding.

What is a Clarifying Question?	
These types of questions do not judge the person talking. They are only for the listener to be clear on what he or she is hearing.	
Example: **Can you tell me more about that?**	**Example:** **You said [x]. Am I getting that right?**

INTERACTIVE

For extra help with Step 4, review the 21st Century Tutorial: **Participate in a Discussion or Debate.**

While the opposite side speaks, take notes on what you hear in the space below.

3. **Switch!** Now NO and YES will switch sides. If you argued YES before, now you will argue NO. Work with your same partner and use your notes. Add any arguments and evidence from the clues and sources. Those *now* arguing YES go first.

When both sides have finished, answer the following:

Before I started this discussion with my fellow legislators, my opinion was that the Senate	*After* I started this discussion with my fellow legislators, my opinion was that the Senate
____ should be based on population.	____ should be based on population.
____ should not be based on population.	____ should not be based on population.

4. **Point of View** Do you all agree on the answer to the Guiding Question?

- ——Yes
- ——No

If not, on what points do you all agree?

Take Notes

Literacy Skills: Summarize Use what you have read to complete the flowchart. For each main heading in the reading, write the important points under that heading. Then use the information you have collected to summarize that section of the lesson in the top box. The first one has been completed for you.

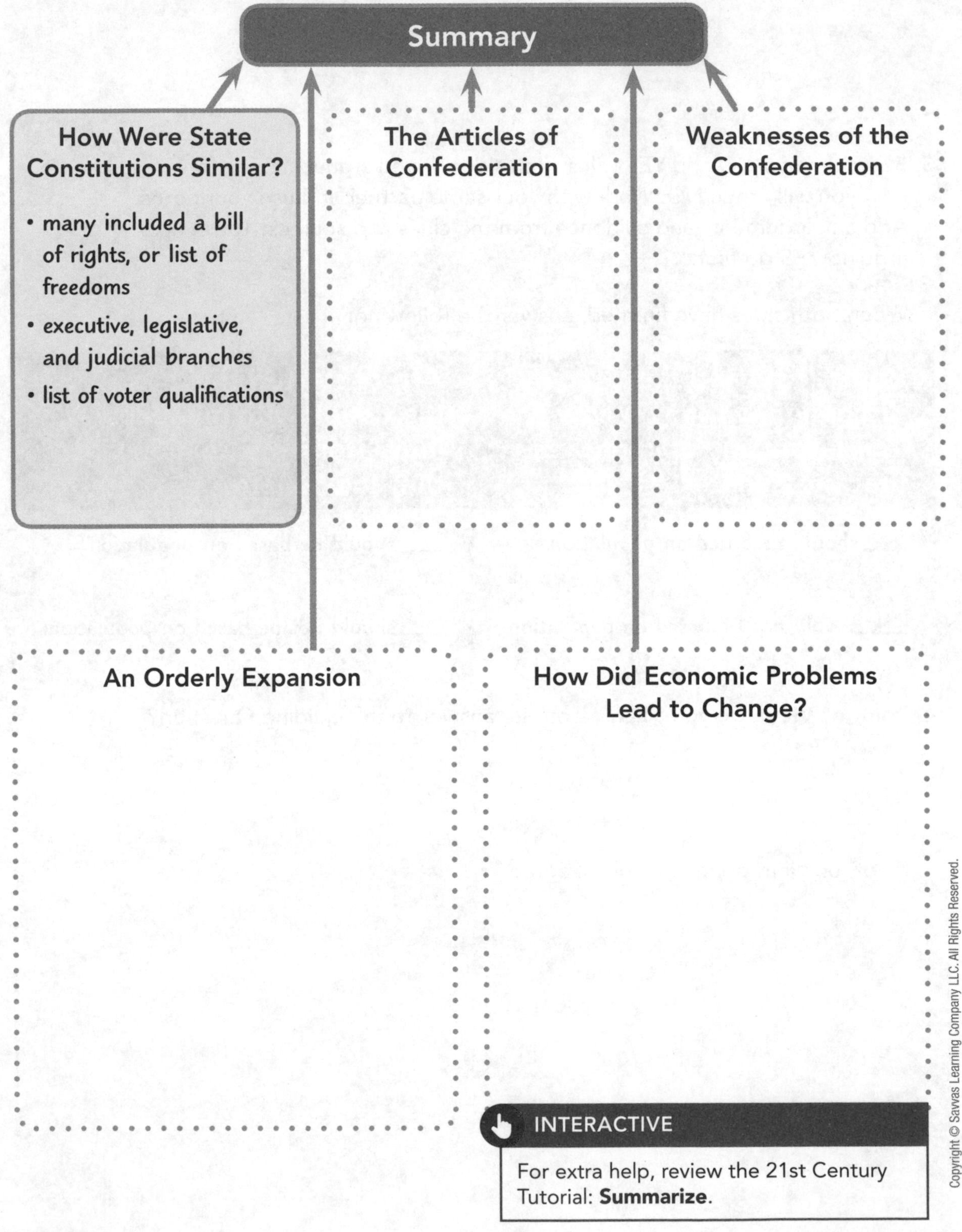
Summary
How Were State Constitutions Similar?
• many included a bill of rights, or list of freedoms
• executive, legislative, and judicial branches
• list of voter qualifications
The Articles of Confederation
Weaknesses of the Confederation
An Orderly Expansion
How Did Economic Problems Lead to Change?

INTERACTIVE

For extra help, review the 21st Century Tutorial: **Summarize**.

Practice Vocabulary

True or False? Decide whether each statement below is true or false. Circle T or F, and then explain your answer. Be sure to include the underlined vocabulary word in your explanation. The first one is done for you.

1. **T / F** States list the structure and powers of government in a bill of rights.
   False. States list the basic freedoms that government promises to protect in a bill of rights.

2. **T / F** A document that sets out the basic laws, principles, organization, and processes of a government is called a constitution.

3. **T / F** The Articles of Confederation was the first American constitution; it created a loose alliance of 13 independent states.

4. **T / F** To cede land means to claim it for your state.

5. **T / F** The Continental Congress authorized the printing of paper money, or currency.

6. **T / F** Shays's Rebellion occurred because leaders from several states decided that the Articles of Confederation did not work.

7. **T / F** The Northwest Ordinance outlawed slavery in the thirteen colonies.

Take Notes

Literacy Skills: Compare and Contrast Use what you have read to complete the Venn diagram. In the main circles, write characteristics of the Great Compromise and the Three-Fifths Compromise. In the overlapping area, write two ways in which these compromises are alike. The first item has been completed for you.

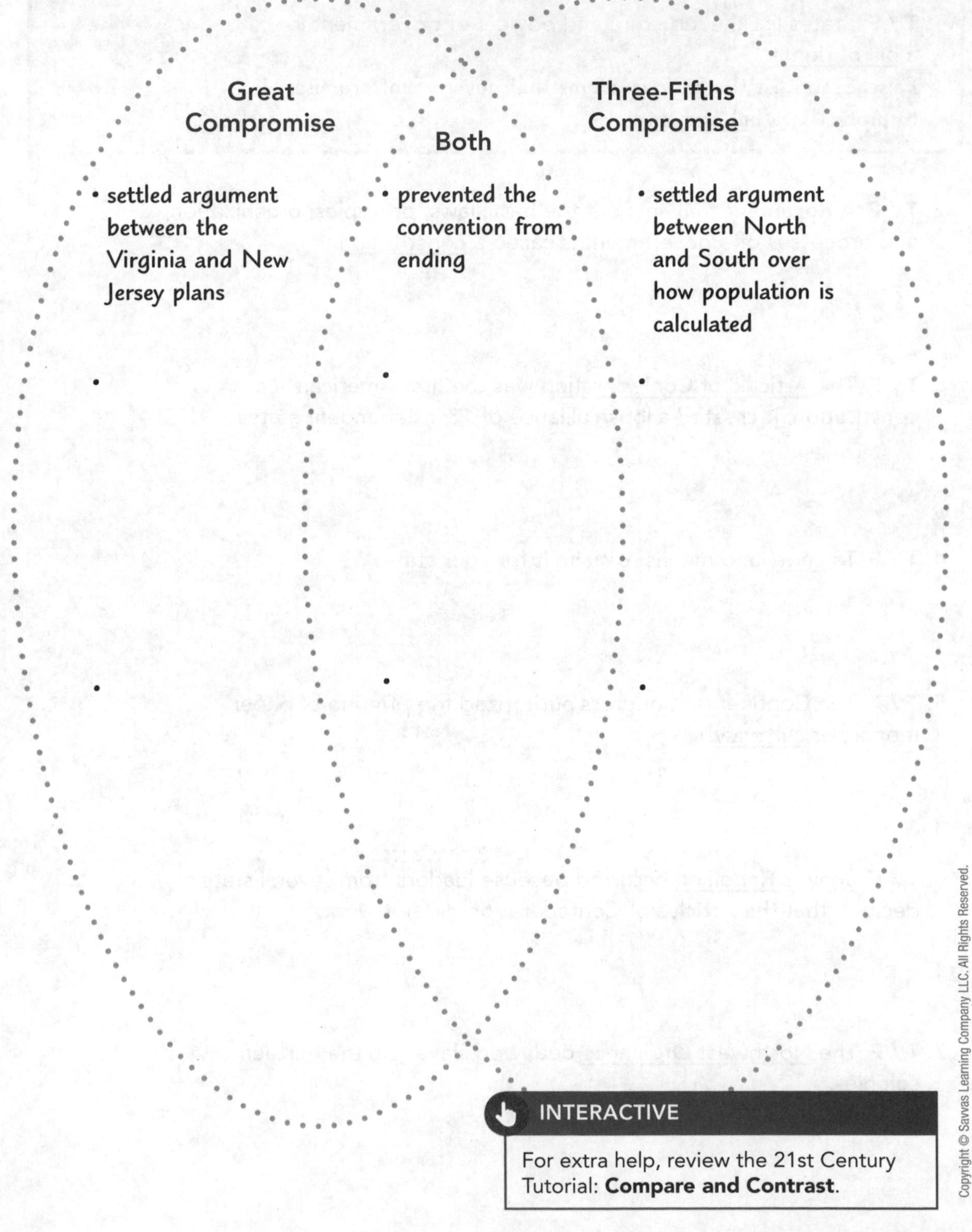

Great Compromise
• settled argument between the Virginia and New Jersey plans
•
•
Both
• prevented the convention from ending
•
•
Three-Fifths Compromise
• settled argument between North and South over how population is calculated
•
•

INTERACTIVE

For extra help, review the 21st Century Tutorial: **Compare and Contrast**.

Practice Vocabulary

Vocabulary Quiz Show **Some quiz shows ask a question and expect the contestant to give the answer. In other shows, the contestant is given an answer and must supply the question. If the blank is in the Question column, write the question that would result in the answer in the Answer column. If the question is supplied, write the answer.**

Question	Answer
1.	1. Constitutional Convention
2. Under which plan was the number of representatives based on population?	2.
3.	3. New Jersey Plan
4.	4. compromise
5. What is the name of the compromise that solved the issue of representation in Congress?	5.
6.	6. Three-Fifths Compromise

Quick Activity Focus on a Framer

With a partner or small group, examine this short biography of framer James Madison.

Did you know?

Often sleeping only four hours a night, James Madison graduated from the College of New Jersey (today, Princeton University) in just two years.

James Madison Jr. was the eldest of ten children. He grew up at Montpelier, a 5,000-acre plantation in Virginia. Frequently ill and painfully shy, at 12 he began studying Greek, Latin, French, geography, mathematics, and literature. Later he attended the College of New Jersey at Princeton. In 1776, Madison was elected to the Virginia Constitutional Convention, where he impressed members with his grasp of political philosophy. He next served in the Continental Congress, and then the state legislature. During this time, Madison spent long hours poring over books of history, government, and law. In 1787, he traveled to Philadelphia as one of Virginia's delegates to the Constitutional Convention. Many years later, he served as the fourth President of the United States.

James Madison's father was a leading landowner in Virginia. What are two other key features of James Madison's background?

The excerpt below is taken from the notes James Madison took during the Constitutional Convention. In it, he is arguing against the New Jersey Plan.

> [James Madison] enumerated [listed] the objections against an equality of votes in the second branch. . . . 1. The minority could [negate] the will of the majority of the people. 2. They could extort [get by force] measures, by making them a condition of their assent [agreement] to other necessary measures. 3. They could obtrude [force] measures on the majority, by virtue of the peculiar powers which would be vested in the Senate. 4. The evil, instead of being cured by time, would increase with every new State that should be admitted, as they must all be admitted on the principle of equality.
>
> — *James Madison, Debates in the Federal Convention of 1787, July 14, 1787*

Team Challenge! What point is James Madison making in this excerpt? Work together to draw conclusions about the relationship between Madison's background and the point of view he expresses in the excerpt. Write a short paragraph explaining your conclusions.

Take Notes

Literacy Skills: Classify and Categorize Use what you have read to complete the table. Write the most important ideas from each group that influenced the founders as they wrote the Constitution. The first one has been completed for you.

Roman Ideas	• *encourage civic republicanism* • *avoid corruption* • *educate citizens*
English Ideas	
American Ideas	
Enlightenment Ideas	

INTERACTIVE

For extra help, review the 21st Century Tutorial: **Categorize**.

Practice Vocabulary

Use a Word Bank Choose one word from the word bank to fill in each blank. When you have finished, you will have a short summary of important ideas from the section.

Word Bank

republic	dictatorship	Magna Carta
English Bill of Rights	separation of powers	

The Framers of the Constitution drew on many ideas as they worked to create a new government for the United States. They looked to ancient Rome, for example, which was a ____________, a government in which citizens rule themselves through elected representatives. They also considered the ideas put forward in great English documents. The ____________ stated that kings had to obey the law and that the nobles had certain rights. Other important ideas, such as the right to trial by jury, were found in a document created in 1689, the ____________. In addition to protecting the rights of the people, the Framers also knew it was important to make sure the new government would not become a ____________, a government in which one person or a small group of people holds all the power. To prevent this from happening, they included important principles in the Constitution, such as the ____________, which says that the powers of government should be divided up among several branches.

Take Notes

Literacy Skills: Sequence Use what you have read to complete the timeline. Determine the date for each of the events listed. Then, draw a line from each event to its correct position on the timeline.

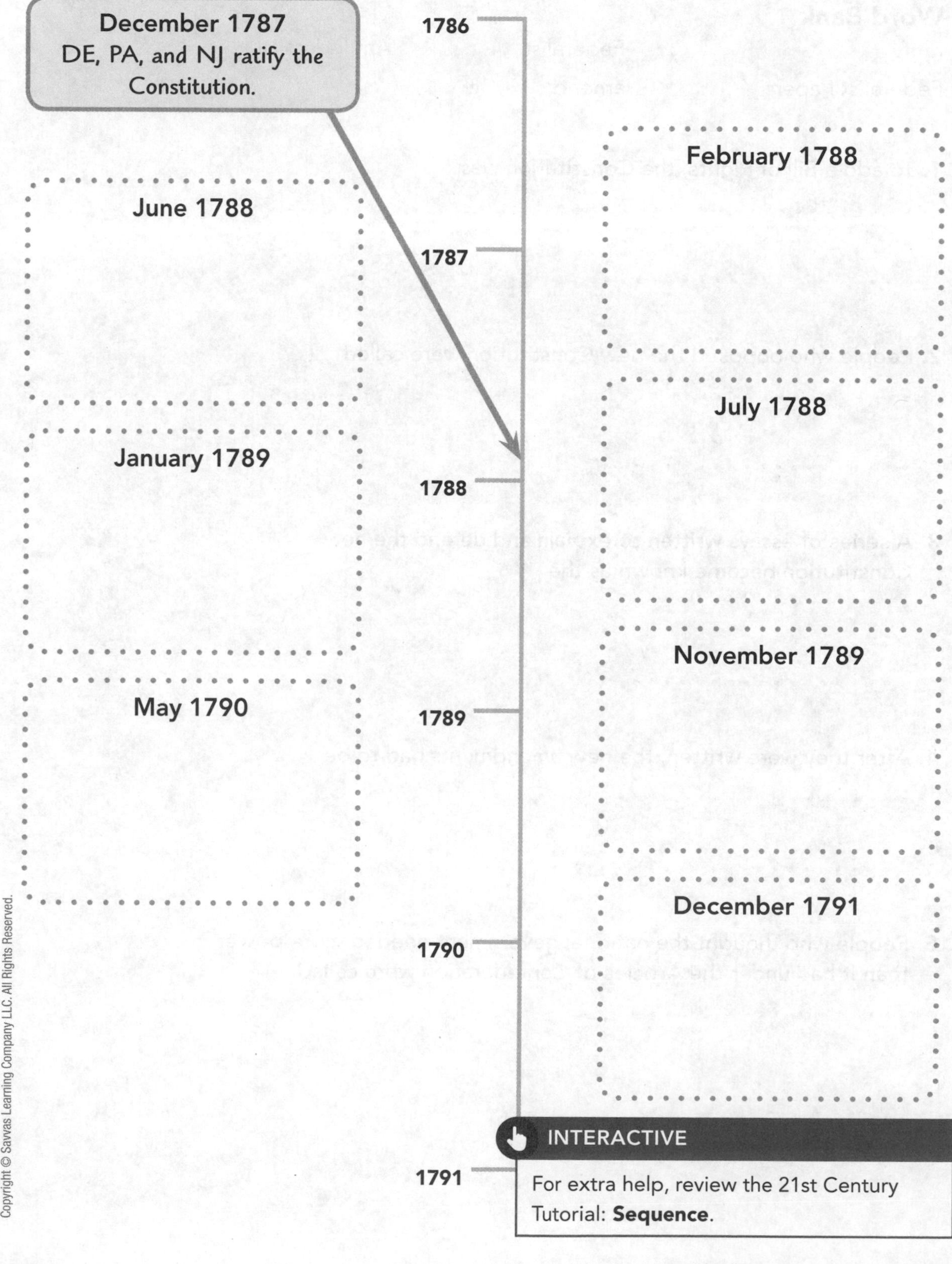

INTERACTIVE

For extra help, review the 21st Century Tutorial: **Sequence**.

Practice Vocabulary

Sentence Builder **Finish the sentences below with a key term from the Word Bank. You may have to change the form of the words to complete the sentences.**

Word Bank

ratify | Federalist | Antifederalist
Federalist Papers | amend

1. To add a Bill of Rights, the Constitution was

2. People who opposed the new Constitution were called

3. A series of essays written to explain and defend the new Constitution became known as the

4. After they were written, the new amendments had to be

5. People who thought the national government needed more power than it had under the Articles of Confederation were called

Take Notes

Literacy Skills: Classify and Categorize **Use what you have read to complete the table. Place each key term under its proper category. The first one has been completed for you.**

Key Terms

Preamble
27 amendments
Preamble
Popular sovereignty
Executive
Vice President and executive departments
Checks and balances
Judicial
Federalism
Seven articles
President
District courts
Limited government
Legislative
Separation of powers
House of Representatives
Individual rights
Republicanism
Supreme Court
Senate

Basic Principles	Constitution	Government Structure
	Preamble	

INTERACTIVE

For extra help, review the 21st Century Tutorial: **Categorize**.

Practice Vocabulary

Word Map Study the word map for the word *veto*. Characteristics are words or phrases that relate to the word in the center of the word map. Non-characteristics are words and phrases not associated with the word. Use the blank word map to explore the meaning of the word *bill*. Then make word maps of your own for these words: *popular sovereignty*, *override*, and *impeach*.

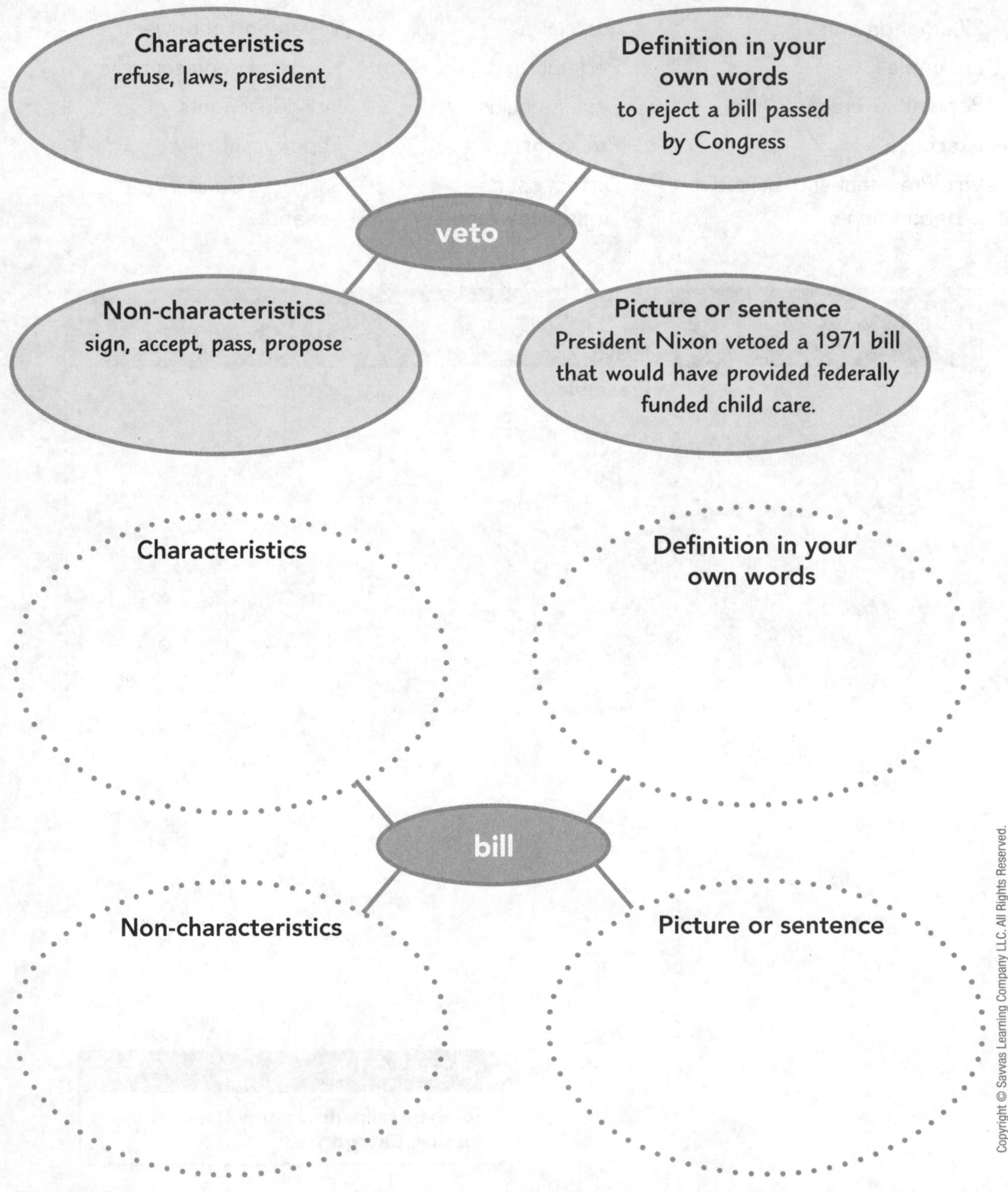
Characteristics
refuse, laws, president
Definition in your own words
to reject a bill passed by Congress
veto
Non-characteristics
sign, accept, pass, propose
Picture or sentence
President Nixon vetoed a 1971 bill that would have provided federally funded child care.
Characteristics
Definition in your own words
bill
Non-characteristics
Picture or sentence

Take Notes

Literacy Skills: Summarize Use what you have read to complete the chart. List the most important points from each section of the text in the lower boxes. Then summarize the entire lesson in the top box. The first section has been completed for you.

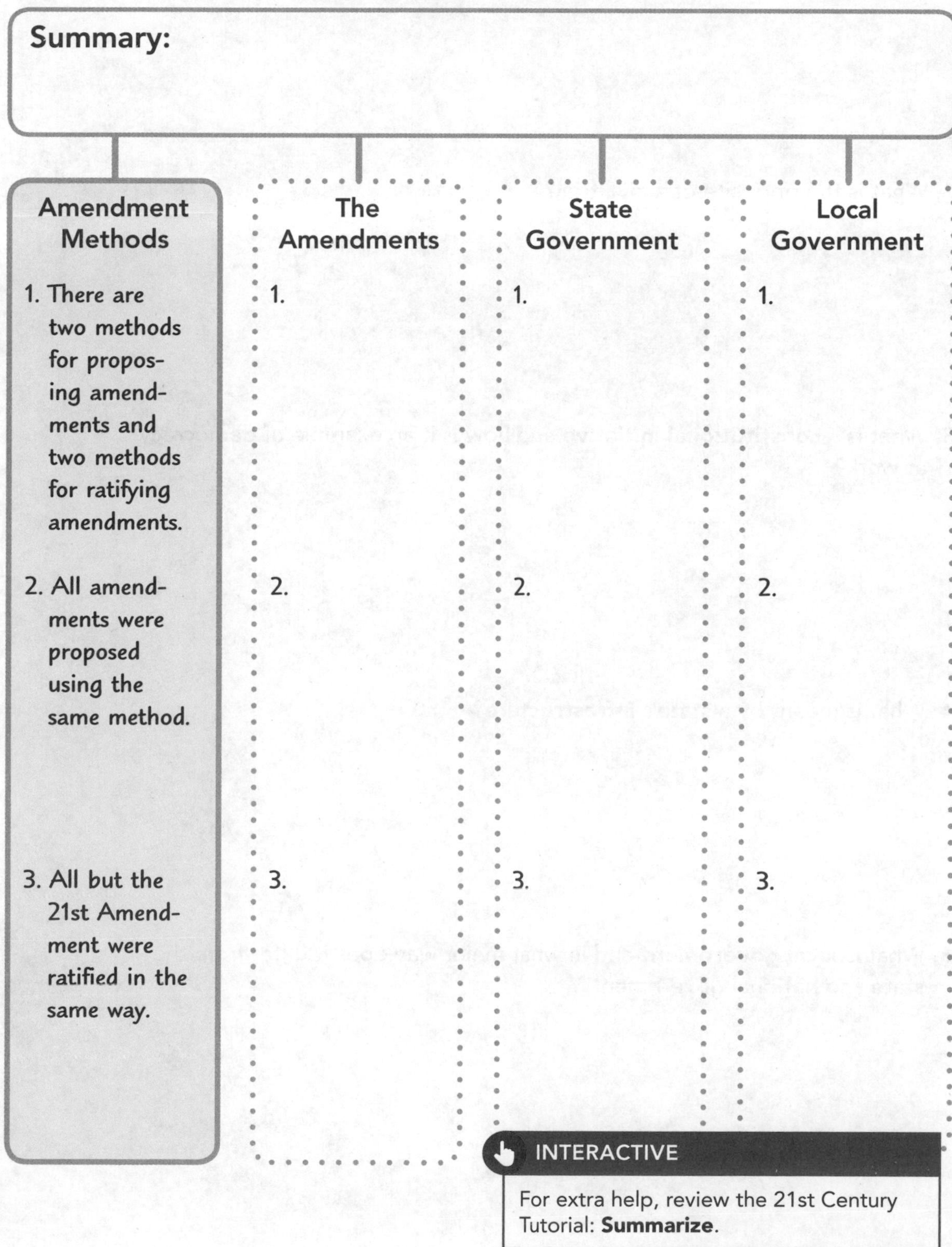

Summary:
Amendment Methods
1. There are two methods for proposing amendments and two methods for ratifying amendments.
2. All amendments were proposed using the same method.
3. All but the 21st Amendment were ratified in the same way.
The Amendments
1.
2.
3.
State Government
1.
2.
3.
Local Government
1.
2.
3.
INTERACTIVE
For extra help, review the 21st Century Tutorial: Summarize.

Practice Vocabulary

Words in Context For each question below, write an answer that shows your understanding of the boldfaced key term.

1. What is the **Bill of Rights**, and why is it important to all Americans?

2. What is the opposite of a **civil** trial?

3. What is a **constitutional initiative** and how is it an example of democracy at work?

4. What is meant by a state's **infrastructure**?

5. What is **local government** and in what major way does it differ from the state and national governments?

Quick Activity Explore Free Speech

With a partner or small group, examine this cartoon related to the Bill of Rights. It was created when George W. Bush was president.

To which amendment from the Bill of Rights does this cartoon relate? What point is the artist making with the signs in people's yards? Why does the man walking down the street say "America the Beautiful"?

> **Did you know?**
>
> Not all countries allow freedom of speech. North Korea, Cuba, Libya, and others restrict the use of the Internet and do not allow citizens to criticize the government.

Team Challenge! Are there ever times when speech should not be protected? Consider the situations below and discuss with your group whether or not each should be allowed. Put a check mark beside the examples of speech you think should be protected.

__blog that criticizes a member of Congress

__book that gives information that endangers national security

__ad that falsely claims a product will make you smarter

__speech that urges protestors to attack the police

__editorial that accuses a governor of stealing money

__burning a cross in someone's front yard

__protestors chanting in front of the White House

__network news story exposing wrongdoing by the president

Take Notes

Literacy Skills: Use Evidence to Support Ideas Use what you have read to complete the chart. Use the evidence in the lower boxes to arrive at a conclusion. Write your conclusion in the top box.

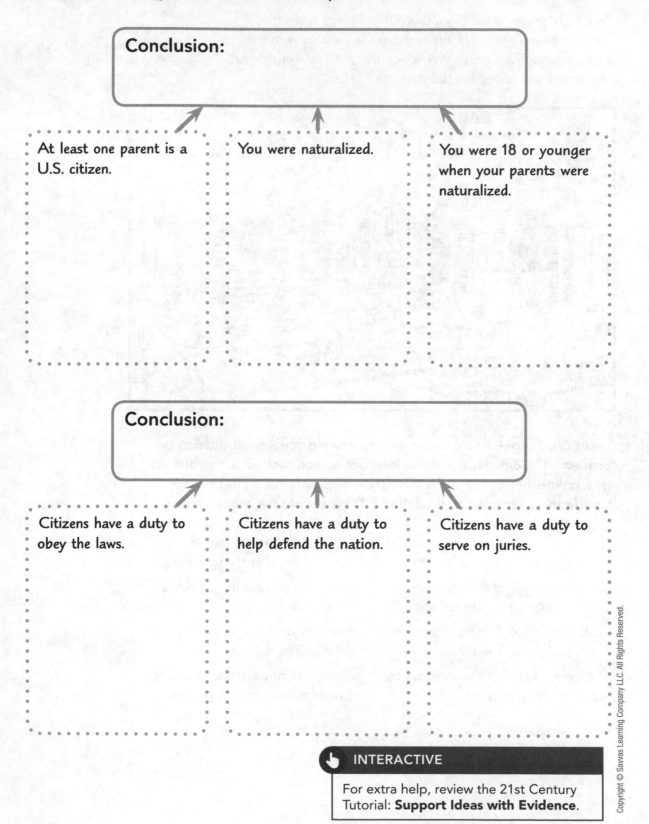

Conclusion:

At least one parent is a U.S. citizen.	You were naturalized.	You were 18 or younger when your parents were naturalized.

Conclusion:

Citizens have a duty to obey the laws.	Citizens have a duty to help defend the nation.	Citizens have a duty to serve on juries.

INTERACTIVE

For extra help, review the 21st Century Tutorial: **Support Ideas with Evidence**.

Practice Vocabulary

Sentence Revision **Revise each sentence so that the underlined vocabulary word is used logically. Be sure not to change the vocabulary word. The first one is done for you.**

1. A citizen is a person who owes loyalty to no particular nation and is entitled to no rights or protections.
   A citizen is a person who owes loyalty to a particular nation and is entitled to all its rights and protections.

2. If you have not yet completed the official legal process for becoming a citizen, you are a naturalized citizen.

3. An immigrant is a person who leaves a country in order to return to his or her country of birth.

4. An immigrant must receive permission to remain in the United States as a resident alien, or citizen living out of the country.

5. Civic virtue is the willingness of the government to grant all American citizens equal rights under the law.

6. Patriotism is a feeling of love and devotion toward other countries.

7. Every citizen has the responsibility to report for jury duty, meaning to decide whether a jury reached the correct decision.

Writing Workshop Arguments

As you read, build a response to this question: **How much power should the federal government have, and what should its responsibilities be?** The prompts below will help walk you through the process.

Lesson 1 Writing Task: Introduce Claims (See Student Text, page 113)

Write a brief paragraph introducing the two sides of the argument about how much power the government should have.

Lessons 2 and 3 Writing Tasks: Support Claims and Distinguish Claims from Opposing Claims (See Student Text, pages 119 and 125)

Based on the information in Lessons 1, 2, and 3, write a few sentences that support each claim about how much power the government should have. Then, for each claim, write a counterclaim. Be sure to use logical reasoning and support your position with evidence.

	Supporting Details	Counterclaim
Claim 1		
Claim 2		

Lesson 4 Writing Task: Use Credible Sources (See Student Text, page 132)

On additional paper, make a list of sources you might use to support or oppose claims about how much power the federal government should have.

Lessons 5 and 6 Writing Tasks: Use Transition Words and Shape Tone
(See Student Text, pages 146 and 155)

Transition words and phrases can help compare ideas (*similarly*), contrast them (*but, on the contrary*), or clarify them (*to put it another way*). Think of more transition words and phrases and write them here. Then, think about the tone you want to take in your argument. To help shape your tone, write a few sentences that reflect your viewpoint about the subject matter, while maintaining the formal style and informative approach required in presenting an argument.

Transition Words	
Tone	

Lesson 7 Writing Task: Write a Conclusion (See Student Text, page 162)

Now that you have formed your own viewpoint about how much power the government should have, write a conclusion for your argument.

Writing Task (See Student Text, page 165)

Using the claims, evidence, and sources you have listed here, answer the following question in a three-paragraph argument: How much power should the federal government have, and what should its responsibilities be?

The Early Republic Preview

Essential Question How much power should the federal government have, and what should it do?

Before you begin this topic, think about the Essential Question by completing the following activity.

1. Write a short blog post that explains how much power the federal government should have, and why.

Timeline Skills

As you read, write and/or draw at least three events from the topic. Draw a line from each event to its correct position on the timeline.

1780	1790	1800

Map Skills

Using maps throughout the topic, label the outline map with the places listed. Then color in the bodies of water.

Louisiana Purchase
land from Great Britain 1783
thirteen states in 1783
land from Spain 1819
Great Lakes
land from Great Britain 1818
Mississippi River

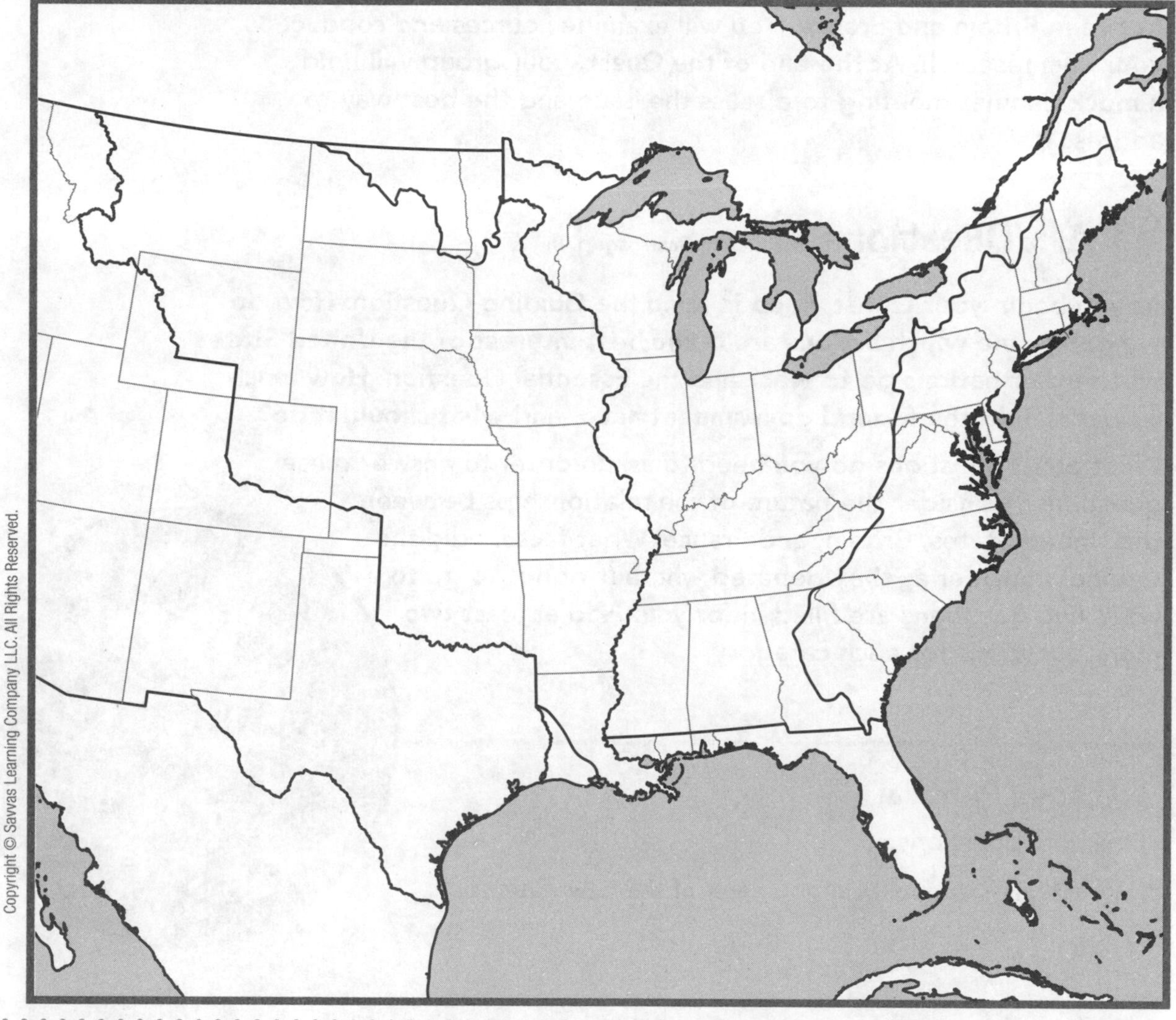

1810 1820 1830 1840

Stay Out? Or Get Involved?

On this Quest, you are working as a member of President Jefferson's Cabinet. The Cabinet must decide how to respond to the war between Britain and France. You will examine sources and conduct your own research. At the end of the Quest, your group will hold a mock Cabinet meeting to discuss the issue and the best way to address it.

1 Ask Questions (See Student Text, page 170)

As you begin your Quest, keep in mind the Guiding Question: **How do we determine which actions are in the best interest of the United States when other nations go to war?** and the Essential Question: **How much power should the federal government have, and what should it do?**

What other questions do you need to ask in order to answer these questions? Consider the nature of the relationships between the United States, Britain, and France. What factors did the Cabinet consider as they debated whether or not to go to war? Two questions are filled in for you. Add at least two more questions for each category.

Theme Political

Sample questions:

What were the political objectives of the new nation?

Did the United States still have obligations to its ally France?

Theme Economic

Theme Relations with Other Countries

Theme My Additional Questions

INTERACTIVE

For extra help with Step 1, review the 21st Century Tutorial: **Ask Questions**.

2 Investigate

As you read about the Early Republic, collect five connections to help you answer the Guiding Question. Three connections are already chosen for you.

Connect to President Washington's Foreign Policy

Lesson 1 How Did Americans React to the French Revolution?

(See Student Text, page 180)

Here's a connection! Read this section in your text. What does it tell you about how the United States reacted to the war in Europe? Why did the President choose this course of action? What did it establish?

How did President Washington enforce his policy?

Connect to the XYZ Affair

Lesson 3 Conflict With France (See Student Text, page 192)

Here's another connection! Read this section in your text. Think about the XYZ Affair and the way that President Adams responded to French attacks on American ships. What do these events suggest about dealing with conflicts?

How did Americans respond to these events?

Connect to American Embargo

Lesson 4 A Ban on Trade (See Student Text, page 211)

What does this connection tell you about the pros and cons of President Jefferson's ban on trade?

Could Jefferson's actions have started a war?

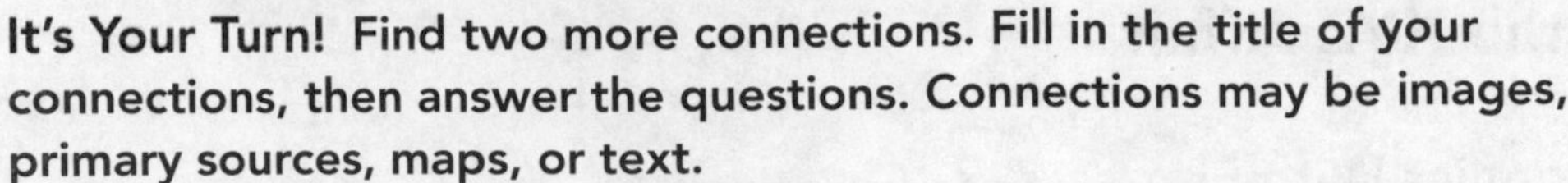

It's Your Turn! Find two more connections. Fill in the title of your connections, then answer the questions. Connections may be images, primary sources, maps, or text.

Your Choice | Connect to

Location in text

What is the main idea of this connection?

What does it tell you about how the United States reacted to war in other nations? What does it tell you about how the United States established its foreign policy?

Your Choice | Connect to

Location in text

What is the main idea of this connection?

What does it tell you about how the United States reacted to the war in other nations? What does it tell you about how the United States established its foreign policy?

3 Conduct Research (See Student Text, page 240)

Explore primary and secondary sources about events leading up to 1793, when war broke out between Britain and France. Fill in the chart to show how these sources provide further information about how we determine which actions are in the best interest of the United States when other nations go to war. The first entry is completed for you.

Source	How do we determine which actions are in the best interest of the United States when other nations go to war?
Washington's Farewell Address	Maintaining a policy of neutrality is the best policy for the nation at this time.

INTERACTIVE

For extra help with Step 3, review the 21st Century Tutorial: **Analyze Primary and Secondary Sources**.

4 Write a Position Paper (See Student Text, page 240)

Now it is time to put together all of the information you have gathered and use it to hold a mock Cabinet meeting with your team to review notes, decide on the best course of action, and document this problem-solving process. In a small group, write a position paper summarizing the chosen solution.

1. **Prepare to Write** You have collected connections and explored primary and secondary sources about how the United States regarded the affairs of other nations. Look through your notes and decide which events and statements you want to highlight in your position paper. Record them here.

Events and Statements

2. **Write a Draft** Using evidence from the text and the documents you explored, write a draft of the position paper based on the outcome of the mock Cabinet meeting.

3. **Share with a Partner** Exchange your draft with a partner. Tell your partner what you like about his or her draft and suggest any improvements you think are necessary.

4. **Finalize Your Paper** Revise your position paper as needed. Correct any grammatical or spelling errors.

5. **Reflect on the Quest** Think about your experience completing this topic's Quest. What did you learn about the United States and its position on foreign affairs in the early days of the Republic? Do you still have questions about the position of the United States on foreign events at that time? How will you answer them?

Reflections

INTERACTIVE

For extra help, review the 21st Century Tutorials: **Work in Teams** and **Make Decisions**.

Take Notes

Literacy Skills: Summarize Use what you have read to complete the chart. Add details related to the challenges facing the new government in each box. The first entry has been completed for you.

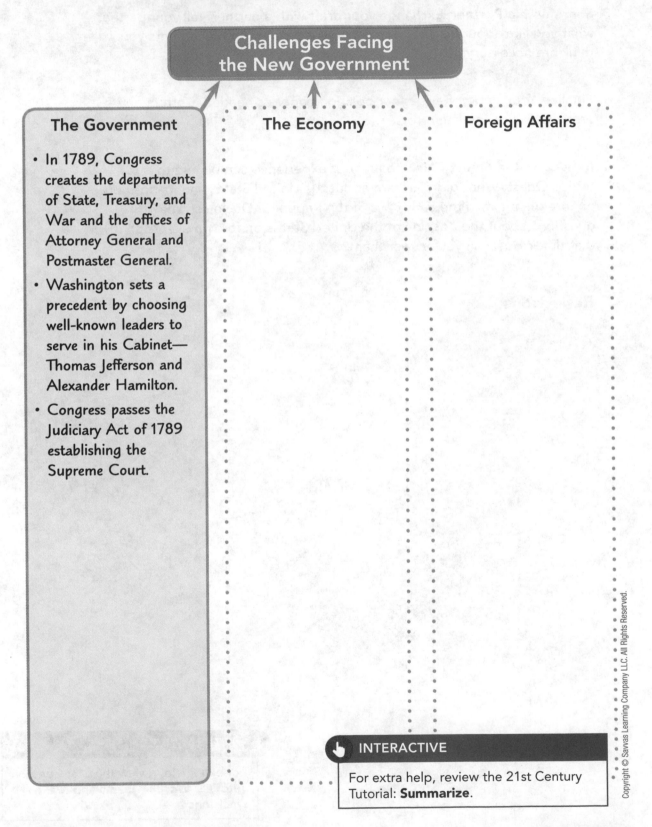

Challenges Facing the New Government

The Government	The Economy	Foreign Affairs
• In 1789, Congress creates the departments of State, Treasury, and War and the offices of Attorney General and Postmaster General. • Washington sets a precedent by choosing well-known leaders to serve in his Cabinet—Thomas Jefferson and Alexander Hamilton. • Congress passes the Judiciary Act of 1789 establishing the Supreme Court.		

INTERACTIVE

For extra help, review the 21st Century Tutorial: **Summarize**.

Practice Vocabulary

Matching Logic **Using your knowledge of the underlined vocabulary words, draw a line from each sentence in Column 1 to match it with a sentence in Column 2 to which it logically belongs.**

Column 1	Column 2
In his first major task as President, Washington chose talented people to fill his Cabinet.	James Madison did not approve of investors making a profit in this way.
Washington's presidency, being the first, established precedents that are still used today.	In 1789, Congress passed this tax on imported goods to protect their products.
On April 30, at Federal Hall, the inauguration of George Washington took place.	The number of executive departments has more than tripled. There are now fourteen executive departments.
Faced with the conflict between France and Britain, President Washington chose to remain neutral.	Hamilton's plan proposed using these to promise payment to citizens.
To help pay off war debts, the government issued bonds with a promise to repay the loans with interest.	In 1796, he decided not to run for a third term. Not until 1940 did any President seek a third term.
Hamilton believed a tariff would help with the new government's debt.	Britain made matters difficult for the United States when it seized cargo from American ships.
Speculators bought war bonds in the hopes of making a profit.	This ceremony starts a new presidency.

Take Notes

Literacy Skills: Compare and Contrast Use what you have read to complete the table. Compare and contrast the political views of the first political parties. The first entry is completed for you.

The First Political Parties	
Federalists	**Democratic-Republicans**
strong national government	limited national government

INTERACTIVE

For extra help, review the 21st Century Tutorial: **Compare and Contrast**.

Practice Vocabulary

True or False? Decide whether each statement below is true or false. Circle T or F, and then explain your answer. Be sure to include the underlined word in your explanation. The first one is done for you.

1. **T / F** The legislative branch has the final word on whether or not a law is unconstitutional.
   False; The Supreme Court has the final word on whether or not a law is unconstitutional.

2. **T / F** The Federalists gained wide support from farmers, southern planters, and workers.

3. **T / F** Differing views on what the nation should become led to factions and the rise of political parties.

4. **T / F** Democratic Republicans favored a loose interpretation of the Constitution.

Quick Activity Take Sides

Look at the political cartoon. Clearly, despite President Washington's warning against political parties, Americans were deeply divided over how the nation should be run.

With a partner or small group, discuss the issues over which Democratic Republicans and Federalists disagreed. Decide whether you would support Hamilton's or Jefferson's views on the role of government.

Team Challenge! **Still working with a partner or small group, list what you consider to be the strengths and weaknesses of having political parties in a nation. Use this list to write a three or four sentence paragraph explaining why you favor or oppose having political parties.**

Strengths	Weaknesses

Take Notes

Literacy Skills: Identify Main Ideas Use what you have read to complete the concept webs. In the first concept web, list the main idea and details of the foreign policy issues John Adams faced during his presidency. The first entry is completed for you. In the second concept web, list the changes Jefferson made to the government during his presidency.

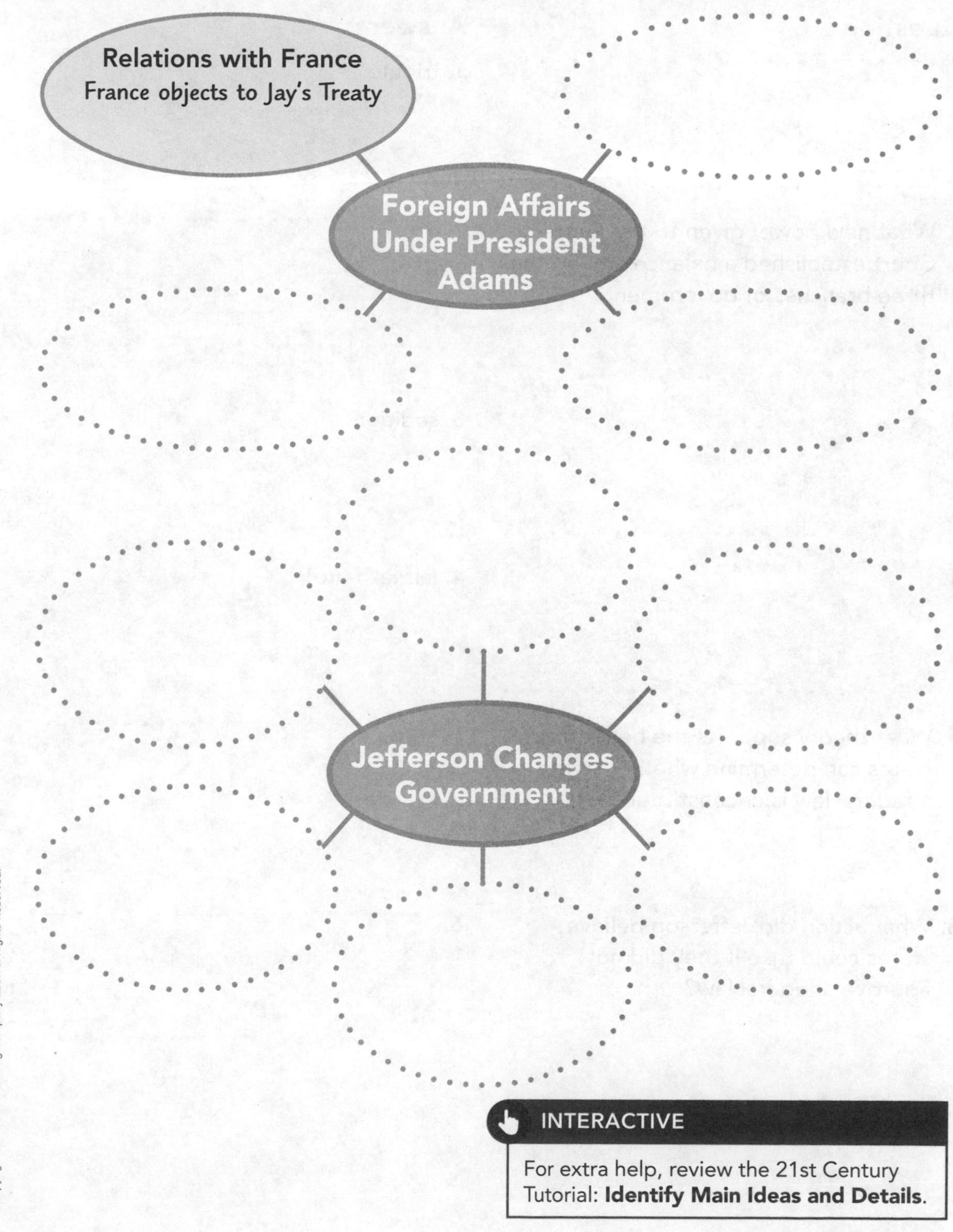

INTERACTIVE

For extra help, review the 21st Century Tutorial: **Identify Main Ideas and Details.**

Practice Vocabulary

Vocabulary Quiz Show **Some quiz shows ask a question and expect the contestant to give the answer. In other shows, the contestant is given an answer and must supply the question. If the blank is in the Question column, write the question that would result in the answer in the Answer column. If the question is supplied, write the answer.**

Question	Answer
1.	1. tribute
2. What new power given to the Supreme Court established a balance among the three branches of government?	2.
3.	3. sedition
4.	4. laissez faire
5. What theory supports the belief that states can determine whether or not a federal law is unconstitutional?	5.
6. What action did Jefferson believe states could take if they did not approve a federal law?	6.

Take Notes

Literacy Skills: Analyze Text Structure **Use what you have read to complete the outline. Add details to explain the significance of the Louisiana Purchase and foreign trade during Jefferson's presidency. The first entries are completed for you.**

I. Jefferson's Presidency
  A. Louisiana Purchase
    1. Buying the land
      a. Western farmers rely on Mississippi River to ship goods.
      b. Livingston and Monroe negotiate to buy Louisiana for $15 million.
      c. Jefferson determines presidents can buy land as part of a treaty.
    2. Exploring the land
      a.
      b.
      c.
  B. Foreign Affairs
    1.
      a.
    2. A Ban on Trade
      a.
      b.

INTERACTIVE

For extra help, review the 21st Century Tutorial: **Summarize.**

Practice Vocabulary

Words in Context **For each question below, write an answer that shows your understanding of the boldfaced key term.**

1. What is the **continental divide**?

2. Why were Americans upset about the British navy's use of **impressment**?

3. What was the significance of the Lewis and Clark **expedition**?

4. What led to an increase in **smuggling**?

5. Why did the **embargo** become a major issue in the election of 1808?

Quick Activity Explore

President Jefferson instructed Lewis and Clark to explore a possible overland route to the Pacific and determine if the Missouri River offered "the most direct and practicable water communication across [the] continent." Jefferson was also interested in the port city of New Orleans, which was a part of the Louisiana Purchase.

With a partner or a small group, discuss why the President insisted on these goals as part of the expedition. Why were rivers so important?

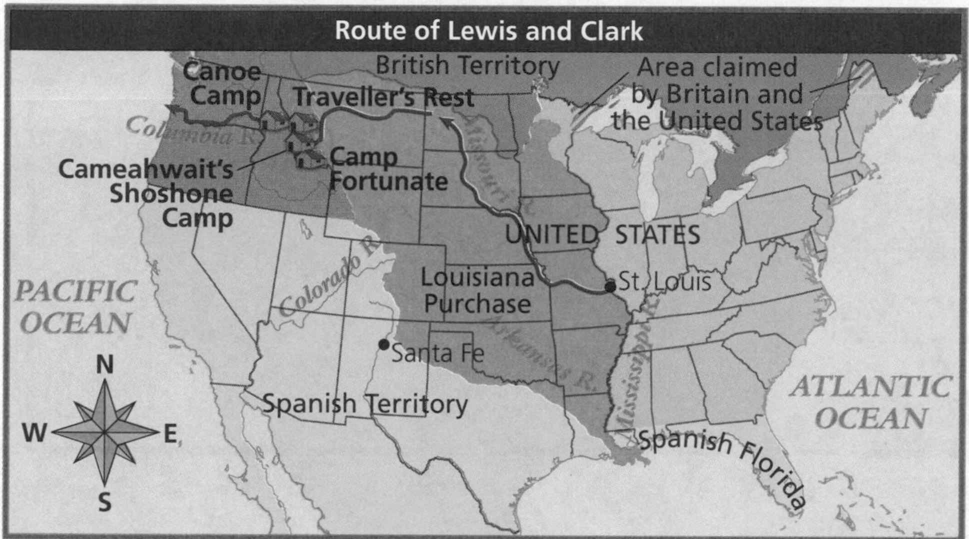

Team Challenge! **With your partner or group, write an entry that a member of the Lewis and Clark expedition might have written in their journal years after their expedition to describe how rivers changed life in the United States. Share your journal entry with the class.**

Take Notes

Literacy Skills: Sequence Use what you have read to complete the flowchart. Provide the sequence of events that led to the War of 1812. The first entry is completed for you.

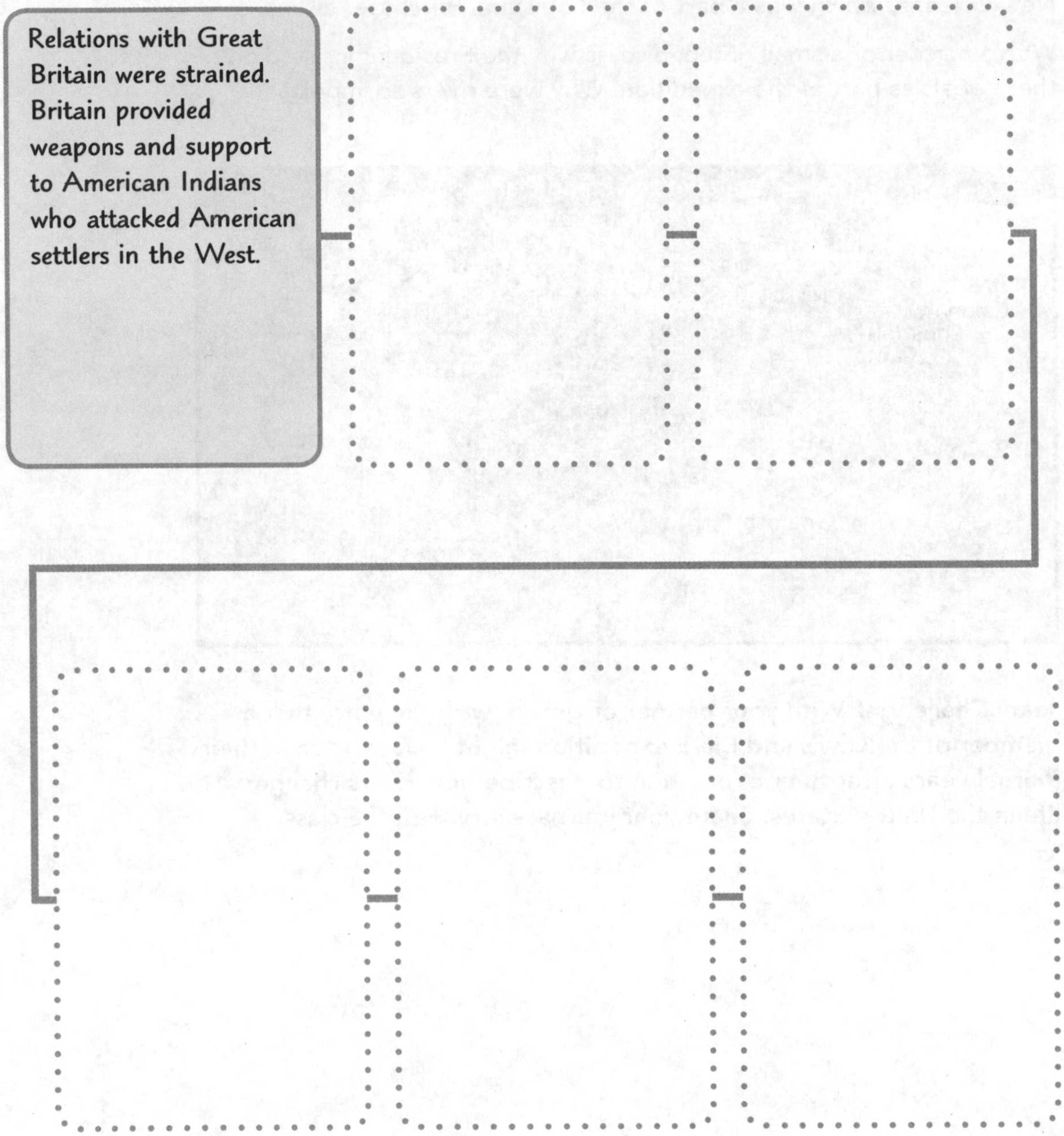

Relations with Great Britain were strained. Britain provided weapons and support to American Indians who attacked American settlers in the West.

INTERACTIVE

For extra help, review the 21st Century Tutorial: **Sequence**.

Practice Vocabulary

Word Map Study the word map for the word *nationalism*. Characteristics are words or phrases that relate to the word in the center of the word map. Non-characteristics are words and phrases not associated with the word. Use the blank word map to explore the meaning of the term *War Hawks*. Then make word maps of your own for the word *confederation*.

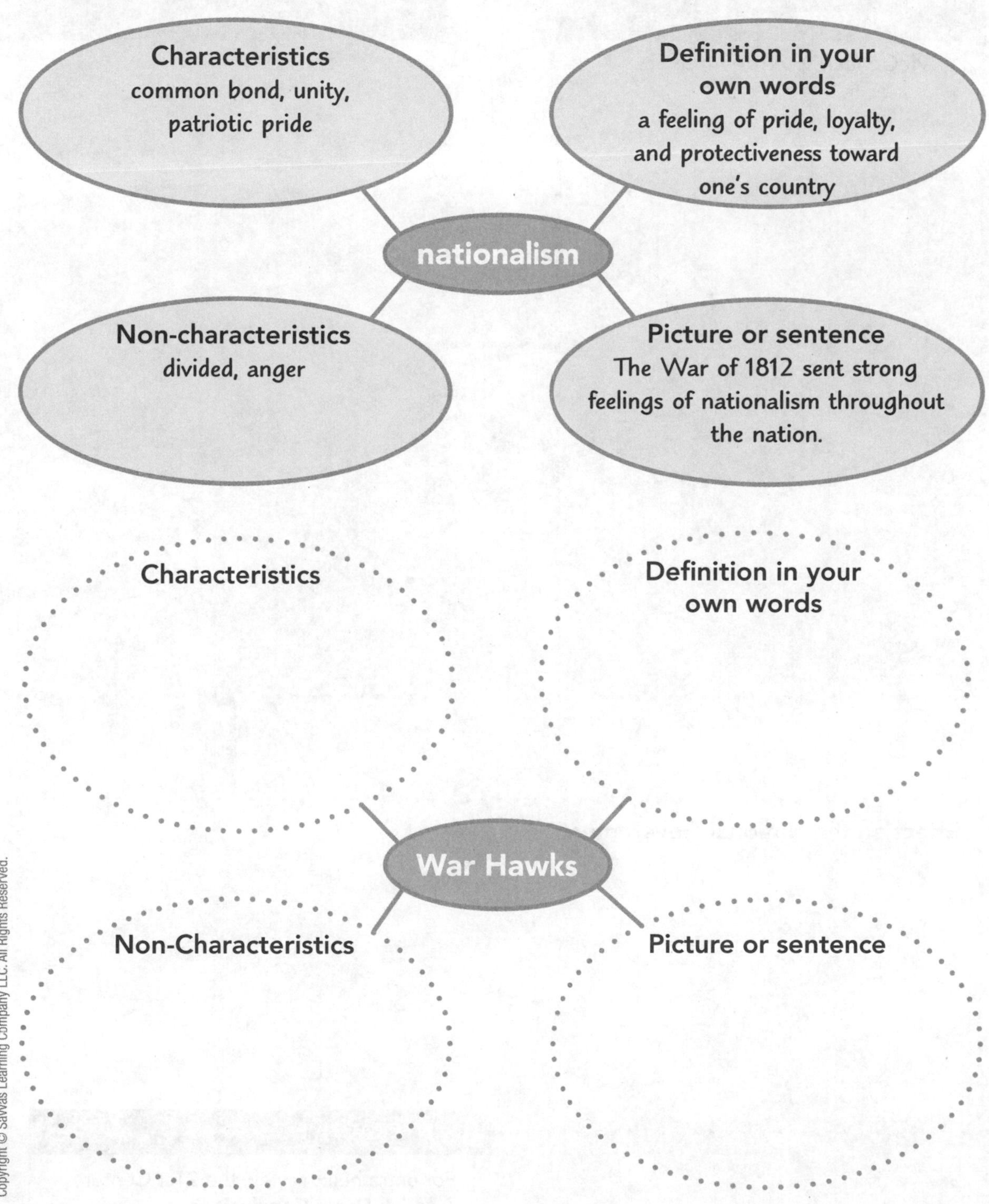
Characteristics
common bond, unity, patriotic pride
Definition in your own words
a feeling of pride, loyalty, and protectiveness toward one's country
nationalism
Non-characteristics
divided, anger
Picture or sentence
The War of 1812 sent strong feelings of nationalism throughout the nation.
Characteristics
Definition in your own words
War Hawks
Non-Characteristics
Picture or sentence

Take Notes

Literacy Skills: Draw Conclusions Use what you have read to draw conclusions about the effect of several Supreme Court decisions on the way the government was run. Complete the flowchart outlining the cases and the decisions. In the bottom box, write one or two sentences about how these Supreme Court decisions affected the U.S. government. The first one has been started for you.

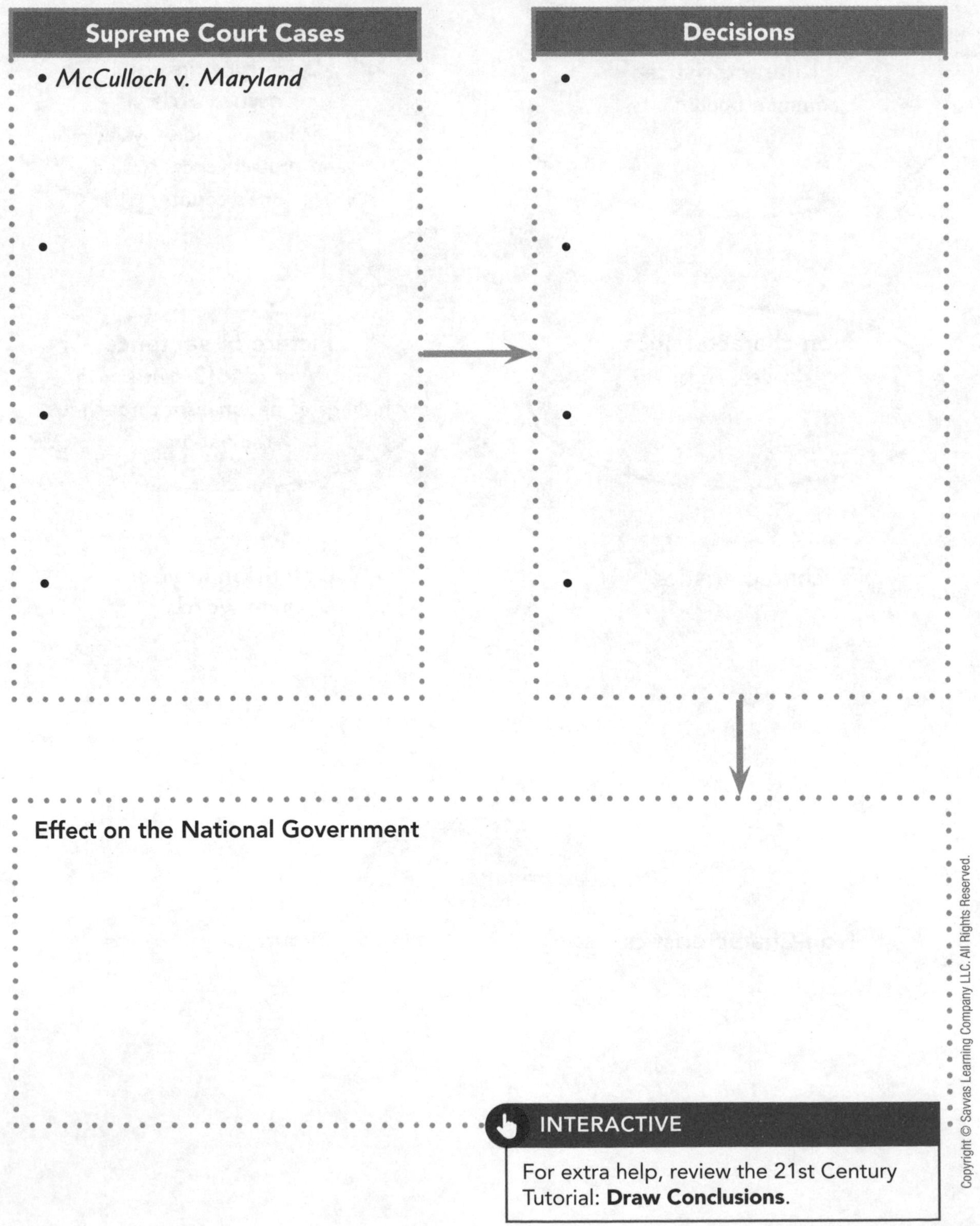

Supreme Court Cases
• *McCulloch v. Maryland*
•
•
•
Decisions
•
•
•
•
Effect on the National Government

INTERACTIVE

For extra help, review the 21st Century Tutorial: **Draw Conclusions**.

Practice Vocabulary

Use a Word Bank Choose one word from the word bank to fill in each blank. When you have finished, you will have a short summary of important ideas from the section.

Word Bank

sectionalism
interstate commerce
intervention
American System
Monroe Doctrine

Nationalism sparked President Monroe's presentation of a plan to improve the economy of the nation. The three-part plan, designed by Henry Clay, was called the ______________. The plan would unify the economy of the states into a national economy. During the Monroe administration, several landmark Supreme Court decisions promoted national unity by strengthening the federal government. One decision, *Gibbons* v. *Ogden*, stated that ______________ could be regulated only by the federal government. At the same time nationalism was uniting the country, loyalty to one's region or ______________ was threatening to drive the country apart. The economy, slavery, and states' rights were major issues. Events elsewhere in the Americas loomed large. Presenting the United States as a world power and protector of Latin America, the ______________ firmly stated that European ______________ would not be tolerated.

Writing Workshop Research Paper

As you read, build a response to this prompt: **Research the country's physical landscapes, political divisions, and territorial expansion during the early republic. The prompts below will help you walk through the process.**

Lesson 1 Writing Task: Generate Questions to Focus Research

(See Student Text, page 182)

At the end of this topic, you will write a research paper describing the country's physical geography, political divisions, and expansion during the terms of its first four Presidents. Make a list of questions that would need to be answered in order to write a research paper on this subject, such as: What were the political parties of this period?

Lesson 2 Writing Task: Find and Use Credible Sources

(See Student Text, page 189)

You will need more information to write your paper. List three credible sources of information you can use to research about the early republic's physical landscapes, political divisions, or territorial expansion.

Lesson 3 Writing Tasks: Choose an Organizing Strategy

(See Student Text, page 200)

How will you organize your research paper? Will you have one section for each topic? Chronologically? Choose an organizing strategy for your paper and describe it here.

Lesson 4 Writing Task: Support Thesis with Details (See Student Text, page 212)

Gather specific details from each lesson that you can use in your research paper. Write those details in the table below.

Lesson 1	
Lesson 2	
Lesson 3	
Lesson 4	
Lesson 5	
Lesson 6	

Lesson 5 Writing Task: Clarify Relationships with Transition Words
(See Student Text, page 225)

What are some transition words that you can use to show the relationship between facts in your paper? Write those words on a separate sheet of paper.

Lesson 6 Writing Task: Visuals (See Student Text, page 238)

What graphics and formatting will you use to help convey information in an engaging way? Make a list on a separate sheet of paper.

Writing Task (See Student Text, page 241)

Using your notes, write a research paper describing the country's physical geography, political divisions, and expansion during the terms of the first four Presidents.

TOPIC 4

The Age of Jackson and Westward Expansion Preview

Essential Question Why do people move?

Before you begin this topic, think about the Essential Question by answering the following questions.

1. If you had the option to move to any city or country in the world, where would you choose to go and why? Include at least three reasons why you chose that location.

Timeline Skills

As you read, write and/or draw at least three events from the topic. Draw a line from each event to its correct position on the timeline.

1820 **1830**

Map Skills

Using maps throughout the topic, label the outline map with the places listed. Then, color in the bodies of water.

Gadsen Purchase	Louisiana Purchase
Pacific Ocean	Oregon Country
Texas Annexation	Mexico
Land ceded by Britain in 1818	Gulf of Mexico

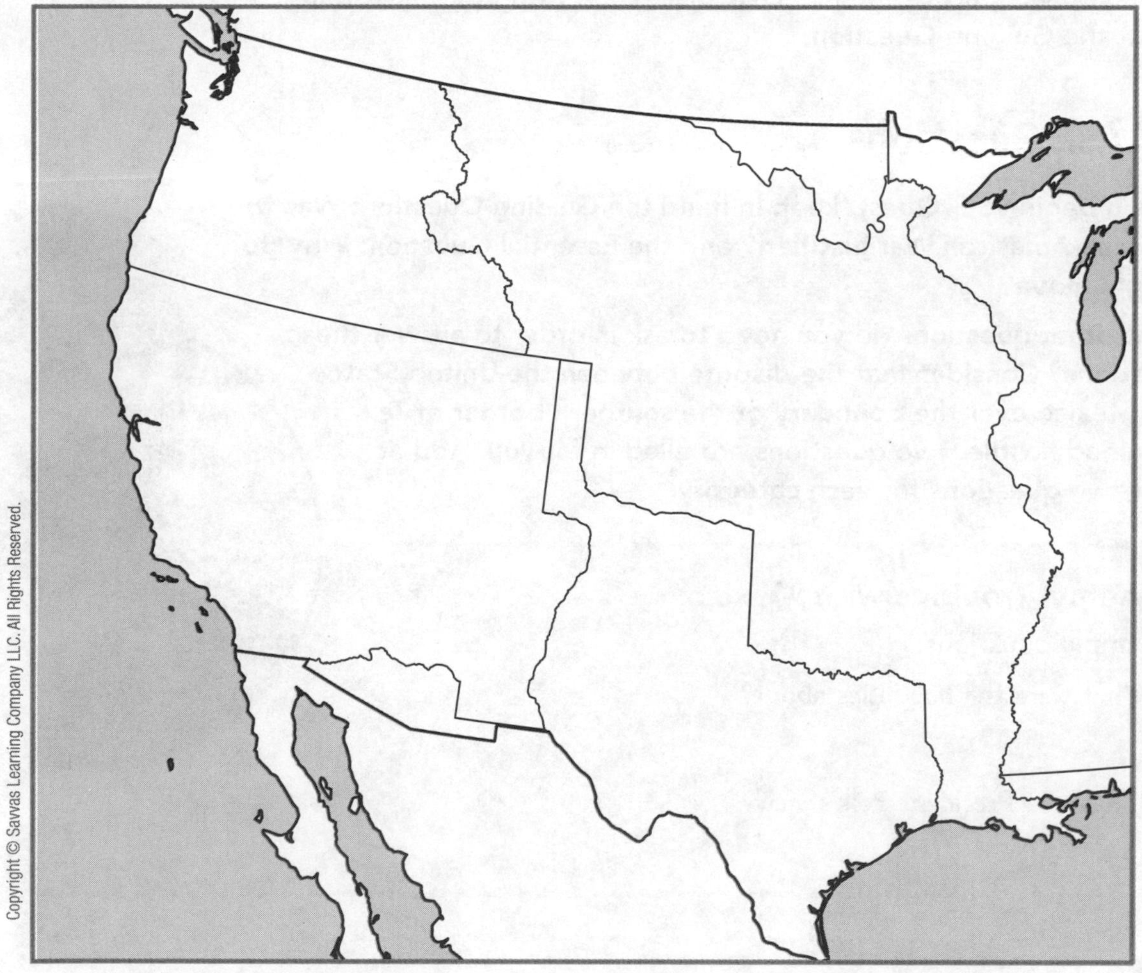

1840 1850 1860

The Mexican-American War

On this Quest, you will explore sources and gather information about the Mexican-American War in the role of a modern historian. Then, you will participate in a civic discussion with other historians about the Guiding Question.

1 Ask Questions (See Student Text, page 246)

As you begin your Quest, keep in mind the Guiding Question: Was the Mexican-American War justified? and the Essential Question: Why do people move?

What other questions do you need to ask in order to answer these questions? Consider that the dispute between the United States and Mexico over the boundary of the southern border of Texas remained hostile. Two questions are filled in for you. Add at least two questions for each category.

Theme Troubles with Mexico

Sample questions:

What were the hostilities about?

What was President Polk's view?

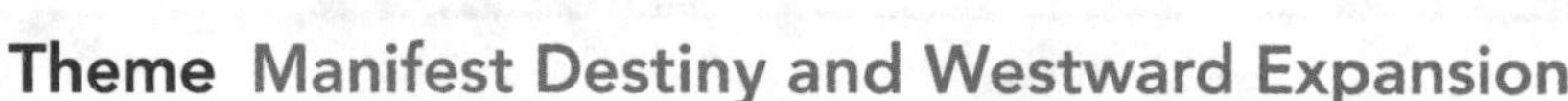

Theme Manifest Destiny and Westward Expansion

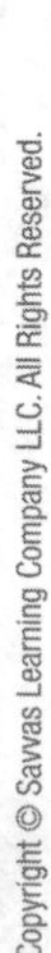

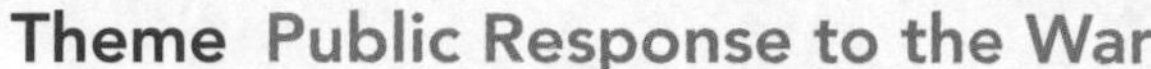

Theme Public Response to the War

Theme Effects of the War

Theme My Additional Questions

INTERACTIVE

For additional help with Step 1, review the 21st Century Tutorial: **Ask Questions**.

Quest CONNECTIONS

2 Investigate

As you read about the Mexican-American War, collect five connections to help you answer the Guiding Question. Three connections are already chosen for you.

Connect to Colonies in Texas

Lesson 6 **Americans Colonize Mexican Texas** (See Student Text, page 296)

Here's a connection! Read this section in your text. What does this event tell you about the significance of Texas and Mexico to the United States?

How did the United States' relationship with Mexico develop after Mexican independence from Spain?

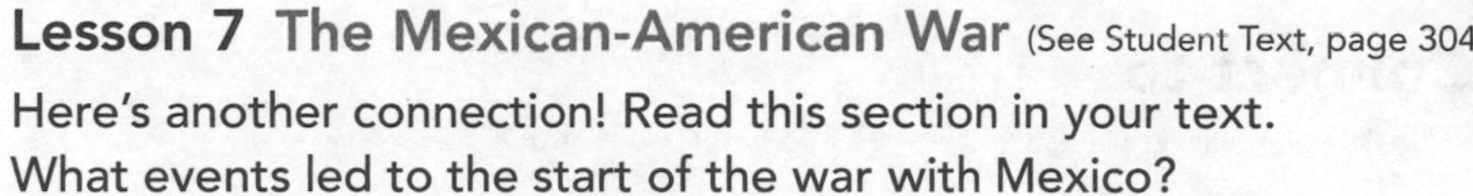

Connect to Causes of the Mexican-American War

Lesson 7 The Mexican-American War (See Student Text, page 304)

Here's another connection! Read this section in your text.
What events led to the start of the war with Mexico?

How did most Americans feel about the war?

Connect to Effects of the Mexican-American War

Lesson 7 Mormons Settle the Mexican Cession (See Student Text, page 307)

What does this connection tell you about the immediate effect of the war's end?

What were the long-term effects of the war for the United States?

It's Your Turn! Find two more connections. Fill in the title of your connections. Then, answer the questions. Connections may be images, primary sources, maps, or text.

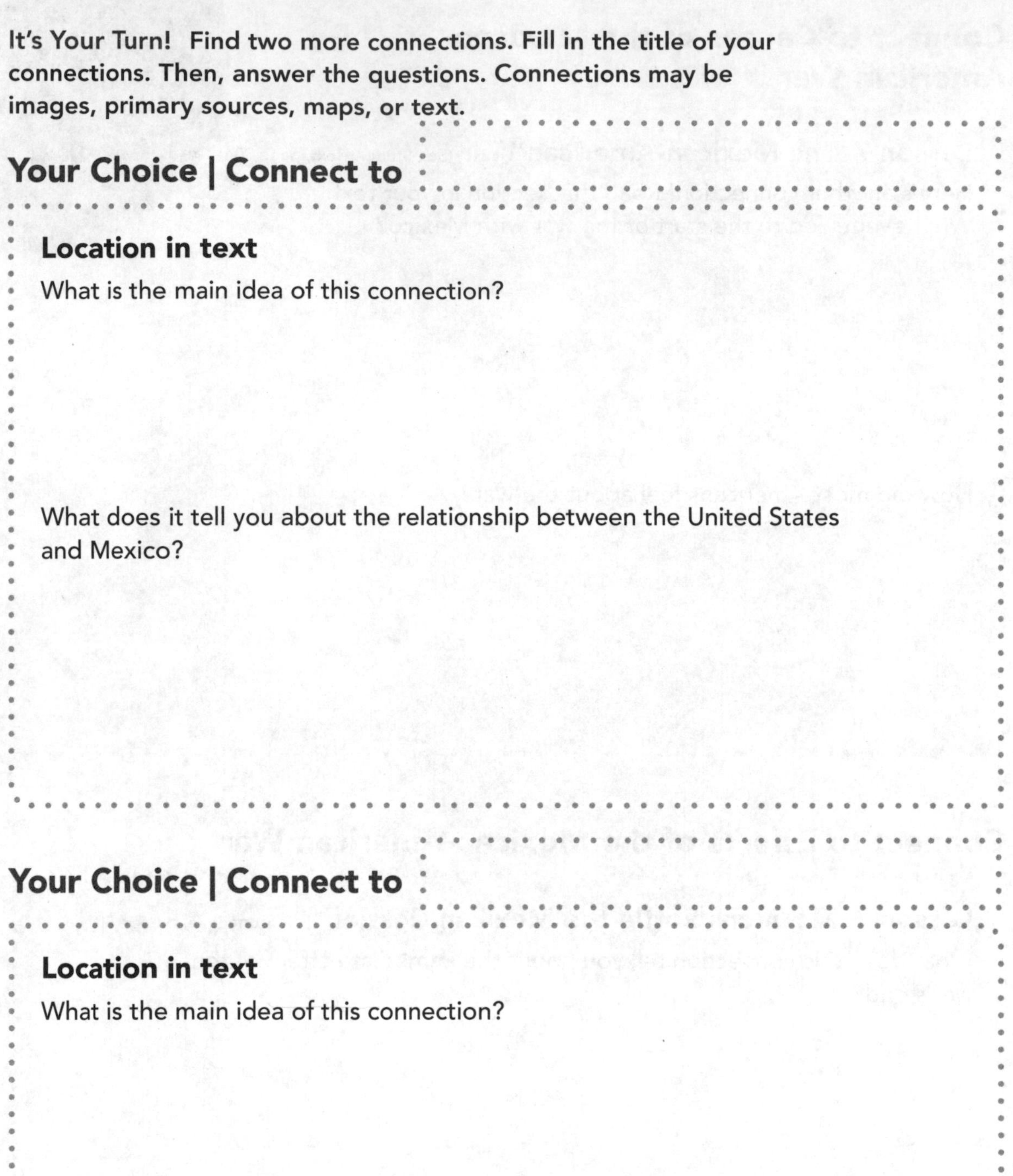

Your Choice | Connect to

Location in text

What is the main idea of this connection?

What does it tell you about the relationship between the United States and Mexico?

Your Choice | Connect to

Location in text

What is the main idea of this connection?

What does it tell you about the relationship between the United States and Mexico?

3 Examine Primary Sources (See Student Text, page 312)

Examine the primary and secondary sources provided online or from your teacher. Fill in the chart to show how these sources provide further information about whether the Mexican-American War was justified. The first one is completed for you.

Was the Mexican-American War Justified?	
Source	**Yes or No? Why?**
"The Borderlands on the Eve of War"	YES. Events in Mexico had weakened the government, revolts were breaking out, there was political chaos and a poor economy. In addition, Mexicans no longer felt a sense of loyalty to the government.
Message on War with Mexico	
The War with Mexico	
The History of Mexico	

INTERACTIVE

For extra help with Step 3, review the 21st Century Tutorials: **Compare Viewpoints** and **Read Charts, Graphs, and Tables**.

4 Discuss! (See Student Text, page 312)

Now that you have collected evidence and explored primary and secondary sources about the Mexican-American War, you are ready to discuss with your fellow historians the Guiding Question: Was the Mexican-American War justified?

You will work with a partner in a small group of historians. Try to reach a consensus, or a situation in which everyone is in agreement, on the question. Can you do it?

1. **Prepare Your Arguments** You will be assigned a position on the question, either YES or NO.

   My position: ______

   Work with your partner to review your Quest notes from the Quest Connections and Quest Sources.

   - If you were assigned YES, agree with your partner on what you think were the strongest arguments from Weber and Polk.
   - If you were assigned NO, agree on what you think were the strongest arguments from Lincoln and Corkwood.

2. **Present Your Position** Those assigned YES will present their arguments and evidence first. As you listen to the opposing side, ask clarifying questions to gain information and understanding.

What is a Clarifying Question?	
These types of questions do not judge the person talking. They are only for the listener to be clear on what he or she is hearing.	
Examples: **Can you tell me more about that?**	**Examples:** **You said [x]. Am I getting that right?**

INTERACTIVE

For extra help with Step 4, review the 21st Century Tutorial: **Participate in a Discussion or Debate**.

While the opposite side speaks, take notes on what you hear in the space below.

3. **Switch!** Now NO and YES will switch sides. If you argued YES before, now you will argue NO. Work with your same partner and use your notes. Add any arguments and evidence from the clues and sources. Those *now* arguing YES go first.

When both sides have finished, answer the following:

Before I started this discussion, my opinion was that the Mexican-American War:	*After* this discussion, my opinion is that the Mexican-American War:
____was justified. ____was not justified.	____was justified. ____was not justified.

4. **Point of View** Do you all agree on the answer to the Guiding Question?
   - ____ Yes
   - ____ No

   If not, on what points do you all agree?

Take Notes

Literacy Skills: Identify Cause and Effect Use what you have read to complete the chart below. List the causes and effects of Jacksonian Democracy on the nation. The first entry is done for you.

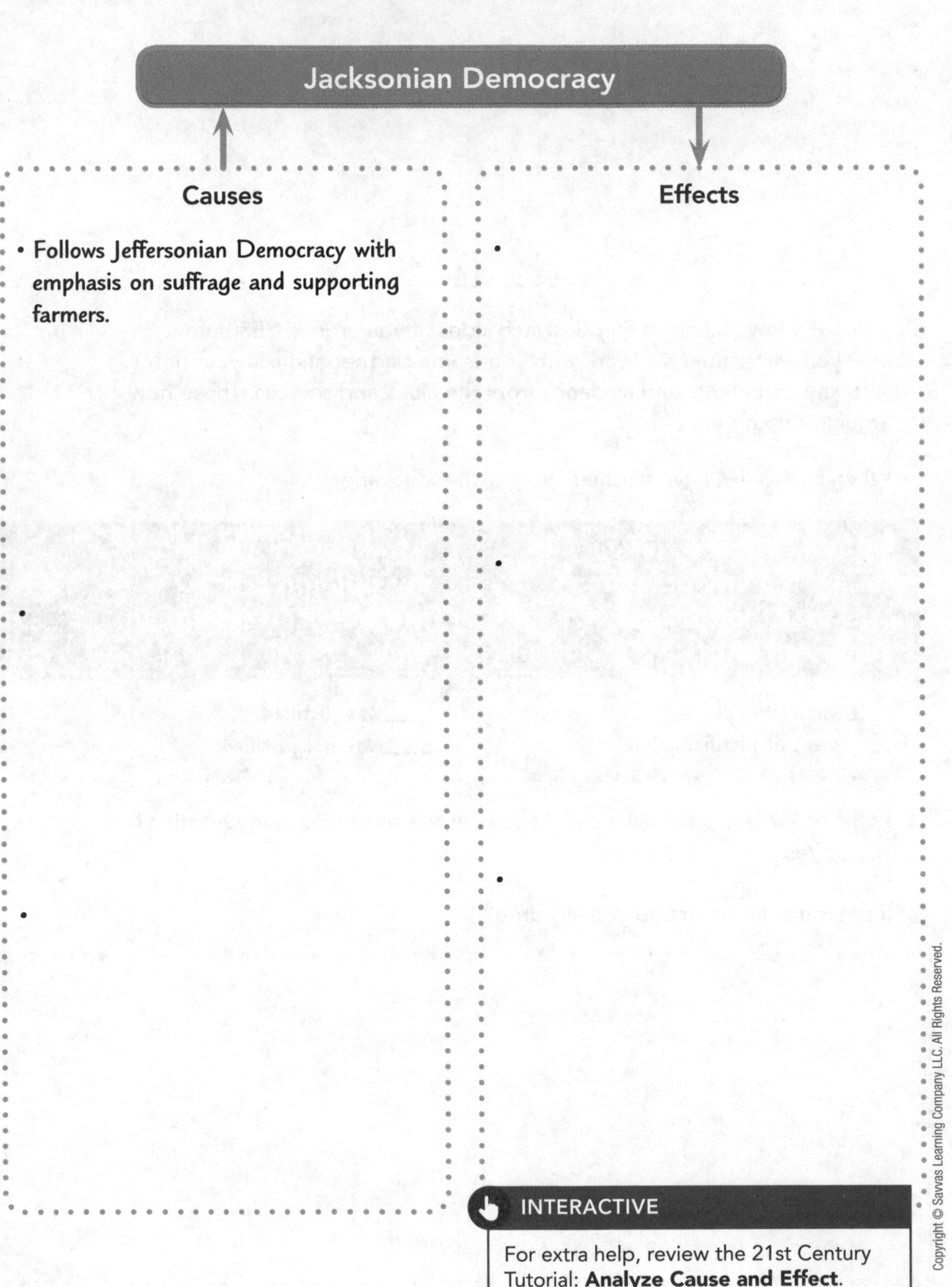

Jacksonian Democracy
Causes
• Follows Jeffersonian Democracy with emphasis on suffrage and supporting farmers.
•
•
Effects
•
•
•

INTERACTIVE

For extra help, review the 21st Century Tutorial: **Analyze Cause and Effect**.

Practice Vocabulary

Sentence Revision **Revise each sentence so that the underlined vocabulary word is used logically. Be sure not to change the vocabulary word. The first one is done for you.**

1. Andrew Jackson's opponents supported the spoils system.
   Andrew Jackson's opponents did not support the spoils system.

2. The spread of political power to the people during Jackson's presidency granted suffrage to women and all males.

3. In the election of 1824, John Quincy Adams won the majority of the popular vote.

4. Members of the Whig Party believed less government involvement improved business pursuits.

5. The Democratic Party platform in the 1830s saw a strong federal government involved in the economy and more privileges for the wealthy as the cornerstone of a strong republic.

Quick Activity

American Equality When Tocqueville arrived in the United States, he wrote, "What struck me during my stay [was] the equality of conditions." Consider the following:

- Tocqueville came from a country where wealthy citizens, or the aristocracy, greatly influenced society.
- Equality at that time in America was different from equality today.

Team Challenge! Work with a partner to create a short "quote" of something Tocqueville might say about equality in America today. Write your quote below and on a sticky note to post for the class.

Take Notes

Literacy Skills: Compare and Contrast Use what you have read to compare and contrast the rising sectional differences among the North, West, and South. Fill in the chart below with information about the economy, federal vs. state government, tariffs, and free and slave states. The first entry has been completed for you.

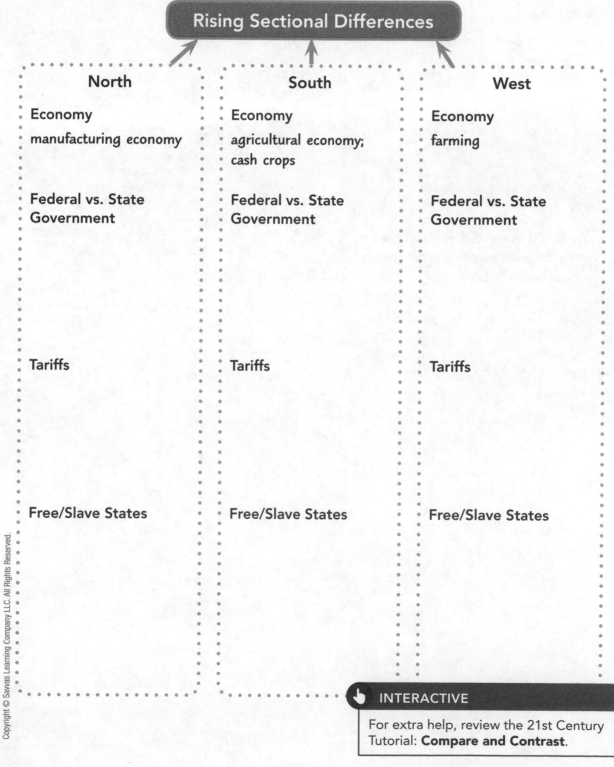

Rising Sectional Differences

North	South	West
Economy manufacturing economy	**Economy** agricultural economy; cash crops	**Economy** farming
Federal vs. State Government	**Federal vs. State Government**	**Federal vs. State Government**
Tariffs	**Tariffs**	**Tariffs**
Free/Slave States	**Free/Slave States**	**Free/Slave States**

INTERACTIVE

For extra help, review the 21st Century Tutorial: **Compare and Contrast**.

Practice Vocabulary

Vocabulary Quiz Show Some quiz shows ask a question and expect the contestant to give the answer. In other shows, the contestant is given an answer and must supply the question. If the blank is in the Question column, write the question that would result in the answer in the Answer column. If the question is supplied, write the answer.

Question	Answer
1. What is a period of severe economic slump and a loss of jobs?	1.
2.	2. states' rights
3. At which event did political parties meet to choose candidates for an upcoming election?	3.
4.	4. Nullification Act
5.	5. caucus

Take Notes

Literacy Skills: Cite Evidence Use what you have read in Lesson 3 to respond to the following statement: **The lives of American Indians were radically changed when settlers arrived.** Fill in the concept web below with evidence from the text that supports the statement. The first entry has been completed for you.

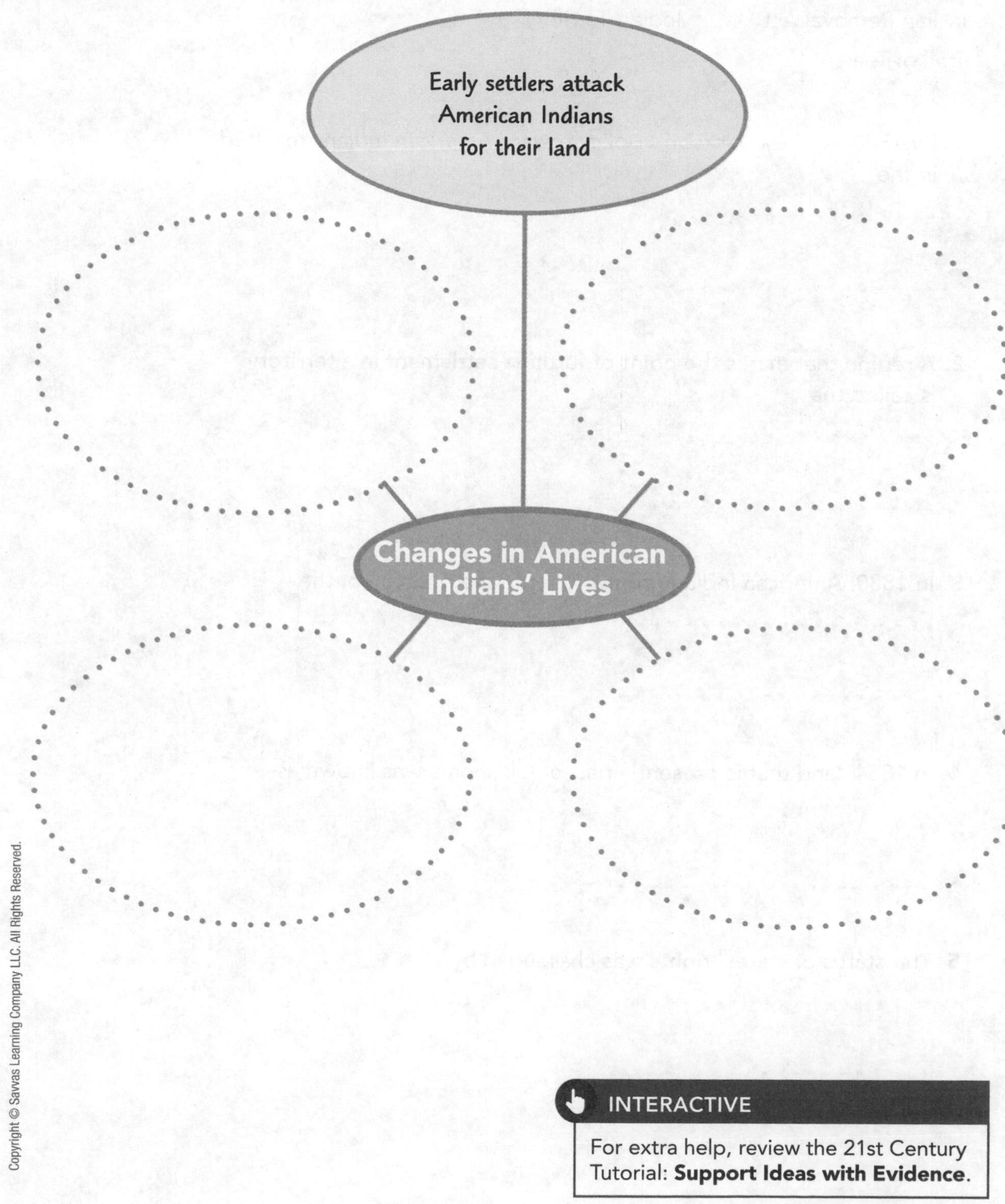
Early settlers attack American Indians for their land
Changes in American Indians' Lives

INTERACTIVE

For extra help, review the 21st Century Tutorial: **Support Ideas with Evidence**.

Practice Vocabulary

Sentence Builder **Finish the sentences below with a key term from this section. You may have to change the form of the words to complete the sentences.**

Word Bank

frontier

Worcester v. *Georgia*

Indian Removal Act

Indian Territory

Trail of Tears

1. By 1838, Andrew Jackson's policy toward American Indians resulted in the

2. A region that marks the point of furthest settlement in a territory is called the

3. In 1830, American Indian groups resisted the passage of the

4. In 1854, land that is presently part of Oklahoma was known as

5. The status of states' rights was challenged by

Take Notes

Literacy Skills: Classify and Categorize Use what you have read to complete the table below about the westward movement. The first entry has been completed for you.

Moving Westward		
New territories	**Why people moved there**	**Life in the West**
Oregon country	Northwest Ordinance opens up opportunities to buy and settle land	farming
Missouri territory		
Texas		
Land from Mexican cession		

INTERACTIVE

For extra help, review the 21st Century Tutorial: **Categorize**.

Practice Vocabulary

True or False? Decide whether each statement below is true or false. Circle T or F, and then explain your answer. Be sure to include the underlined vocabulary word in your explanation. The first one is done for you.

1. **T / F** As the first steam-powered boats, flatboats helped to revolutionize travel and trade.
   False: Flatboats were not steam powered and were used to transport wagons and people along rivers.

2. **T / F** The National Road was the first step in a federal government-funded transportation system.

3. **T / F** The Constitution states that all revenue or income collected by the government should originate in the House of Representatives.

4. **T / F** As canals became important in American travel, *Clermont* became the first canal for transporting goods.

5. **T / F** In spite of high expectations, the Erie Canal failed to improve water transportation and trade between New York City and Buffalo, New York.

Take Notes

Literacy Skills: Summarize Use what you have read to complete the outline below. For each main idea, provide the details needed to write a summary of the topic. The main idea and details for the first entry have been completed for you.

Settling Oregon

I. Exploring the territory
   a. geography
   b. weather
   c. how the land was explored

II. Who came to the area?
   a.
   b.
   c.

III. The fur trade
   a.
   b.

IV. Negotiations with Britain
   a.

INTERACTIVE

For extra help, review the 21st Century Tutorial: **Summarize**.

Practice Vocabulary

Use a Word Bank Choose one term from the word bank to fill in each blank. When you have finished, you will have a short summary of important ideas from the section.

Word Bank

Oregon Country	mountain men
Oregon Trail	rugged individualists

Between 1800 and 1840, thousands of settlers poured into ______________. While the rich, virgin soil drew many, there was also a prosperous fur trade. Fur companies often hired fur trappers who became known as ______________. Many people admired them as ______________. When the fur trade declined, many ______________ hired themselves out as guides along the ______________.

Take Notes

Literacy Skills: Sequence Use what you have read to complete the flowchart below. In each space, write the events that led to the independence of Texas. The first event is filled in for you.

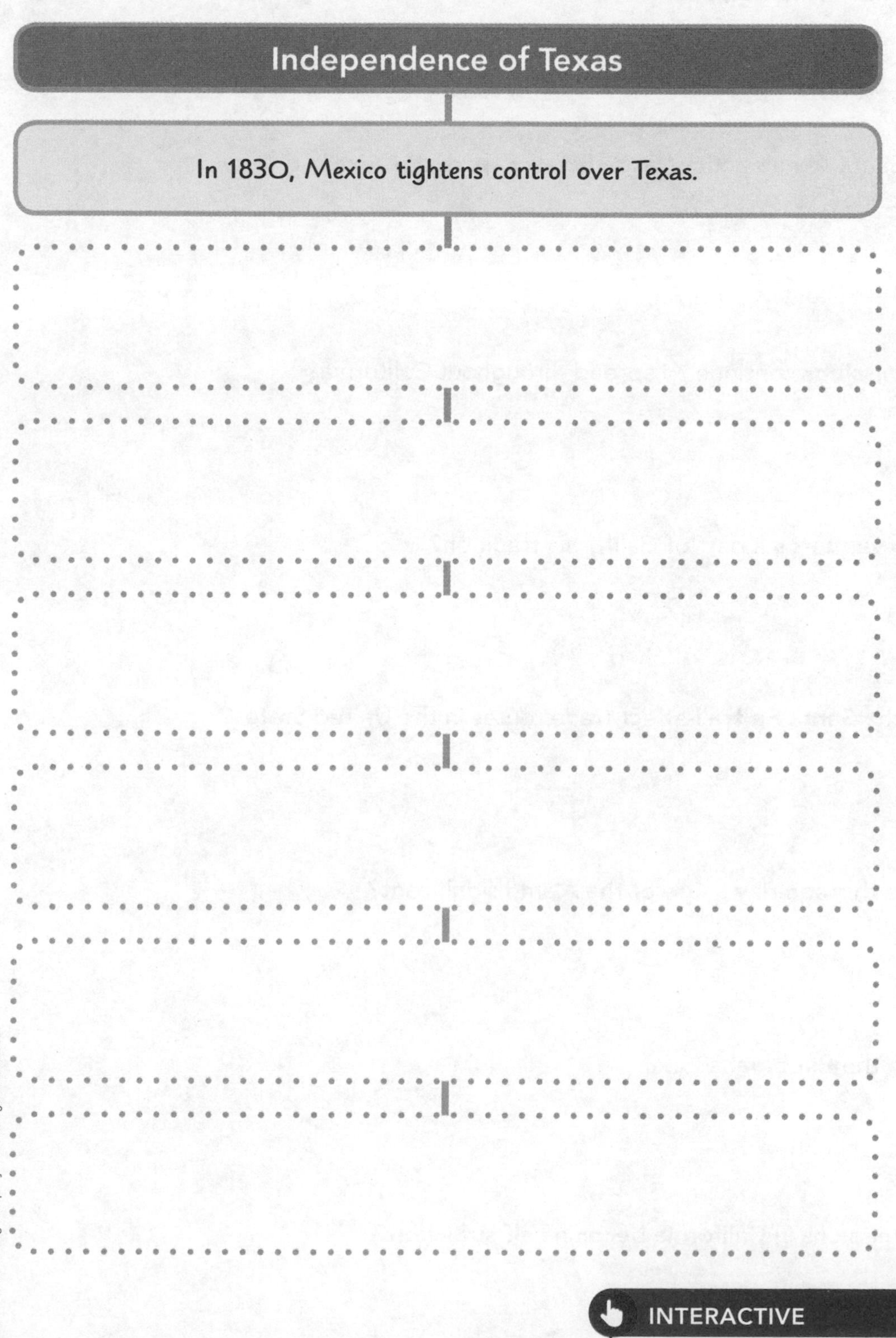

Independence of Texas
In 1830, Mexico tightens control over Texas.

INTERACTIVE

For extra help, review the 21st Century Tutorial: **Sequence**.

Practice Vocabulary

Words in Context For each question below, write an answer that shows your understanding of the **boldfaced** key term.

1. Why was the **Alamo** significant?

2. How did Santa Anna's actions as a **dictator** spark the Texas fight for independence?

3. Why did **missions** continue to spread throughout California?

4. Why were **vaqueros** a part of California tradition?

5. How did the **Santa Fe trail** affect trade routes in the United States?

6. Why is the thirteen-day **seige** of the Alamo significant?

7. Who were the **Puebloans**?

8. How did missions in California become **self-sufficient**?

Take Notes

Literacy Skills: Identify Cause and Effect **Use what you have read to complete the chart below. In each box, write the effects of the expansion of the West between 1840 and 1870. The first entry is done for you.**

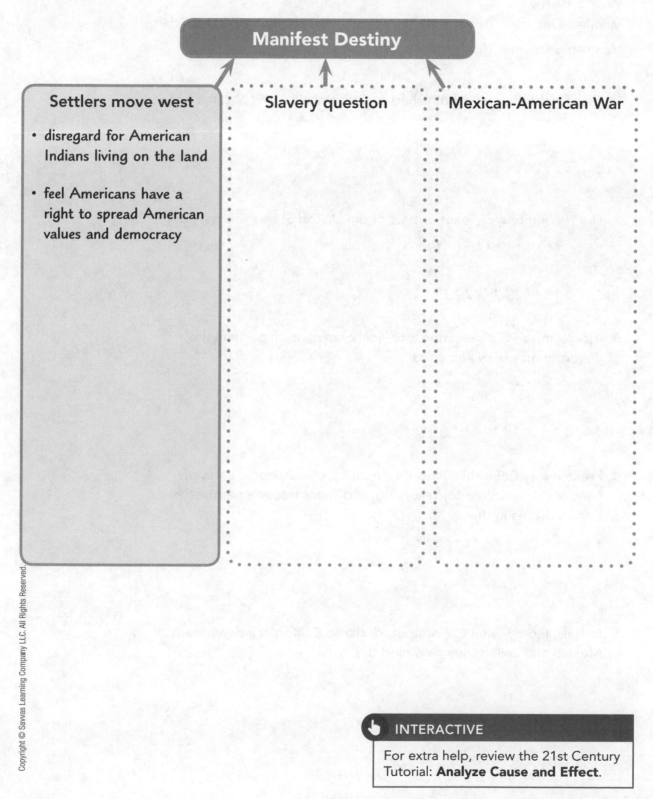

Manifest Destiny

Settlers move west	Slavery question	Mexican-American War
• disregard for American Indians living on the land • feel Americans have a right to spread American values and democracy		

INTERACTIVE

For extra help, review the 21st Century Tutorial: **Analyze Cause and Effect**.

Practice Vocabulary

Sentence Builder **Finish the sentences below with a key term from this section. You may have to change the form of the words to complete the sentences.**

Word Bank

Manifest Destiny | Bear Flag Republic | Treaty of Guadalupe-Hidalgo
Mexican Cession | forty-niner

1. These gold seekers, who rushed to California in 1849, became known as

2. The recognition of Texas as part of the United States was part of

3. After James Polk's election, the goal of expansion became the government policy known as

4. Present-day California, Nevada, Utah, most of Arizona, parts of New Mexico, Colorado, Wyoming, and Texas became part of the United States in the

5. Rebels, led by John C. Fremont, declared California independent of Mexico and called their new land the

Quick Activity The Importance of Water

With a partner, study the photo of the miners seeking gold during the California Gold Rush. What does it tell you about water shortages in the West?

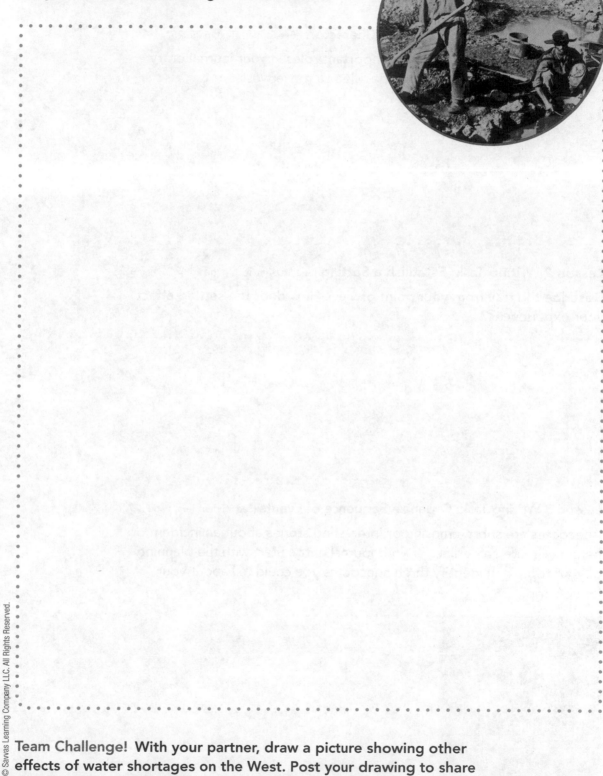

Team Challenge! With your partner, draw a picture showing other effects of water shortages on the West. Post your drawing to share with the class. Explain the message behind your drawing.

Writing Workshop Narrative Essay

As you read, build a response to this prompt: It is 1844 and your family has decided to move to Oregon. Write a journal entry describing the trip. The prompts below will help walk you through the process.

Lesson 1 Writing Task: Introduce Characters (See Student Text, page 257)

List the characters who will play important roles in your journal entry and explain why your family has decided to move west.

Lesson 2 Writing Task: Establish a Setting (See Student Text, page 268)

Describe the trail from your point of view. How does the setting affect your experiences?

Lesson 3 Writing Task: Organize Sequence of Events (See Student Text, page 277)

Anecdotes are short, amusing or interesting stories about an incident or person. Create an outline for your journal entry. Start with the planning of your trip. Then identify three anecdotes you could tell about your family's trip.

Planning for Trip	
Anecdotes	

Lessons 4 and 5 Writing Tasks: Narrative Techniques A good journal entry will use narrative techniques—such as dialogue, description, and similes—to make it more lively and interesting to read. Identify a narrative technique, and write a sentence based on the lesson's content that uses that technique.

Lesson 6 Writing Task: Descriptive Details and Sensory Language Choose one of your anecdotes. Is it interesting enough? Rewrite it, adding descriptive details or sensory language.

Lesson 7 Writing Task: Strong Conclusion How will your journal entry end? Draft an ending for your entry that will be memorable for your readers.

Writing Task Using the characters, setting, and anecdotes you've identified, write a journal entry about your family's trip to Oregon. Be sure to use narrative techniques, descriptive details, and sensory language in your writing. Capture the readers' attention in your opening, and end with a strong conclusion to your entry.

TOPIC 5

Society and Culture Before the Civil War Preview

Essential Question Why is culture important?

Before you begin this topic, think about the Essential Question by completing the following activity.

135,000 SETS, 270,000 VOLUMES SOLD.
UNCLE TOM'S CABIN
FOR SALE HERE.
AN EDITION FOR THE MILLION, COMPLETE IN 1 Vol., PRICE 37 1-2 CENTS.
" " IN GERMAN, IN 1 Vol., PRICE 50 CENTS.
" " IN 2 Vols., CLOTH, 6 PLATES, PRICE $1.50.
SUPERB ILLUSTRATED EDITION, IN 1 Vol., WITH 153 ENGRAVINGS,
PRICES FROM $2.50 TO $5.00.
The Greatest Book of the Age.

1. Think of one way that music, art, or books have inspired you. Then think of one song, piece of art, or book that an artist created because of something happening in the world. For example, *Uncle Tom's Cabin* is a novel by Harriet Beecher Stowe that was inspired by the evils of slavery.

The [song, art, book] inspired me to

The [song, art, book] was inspired by

Timeline Skills

As you read, write and/or draw at least three events from the topic. Draw a line from each event to its correct position on the timeline.

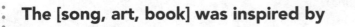

1810	1820	1830

Map Skills

Using maps throughout the topic, label the outline map showing the various travel times from New York City. Then, create a key for each of the various travel times and use the key to color the map.

1 day, 1857	1 week, 1857	4 weeks, 1857
1 day, 1800	1 week, 1800	4 weeks, 1800

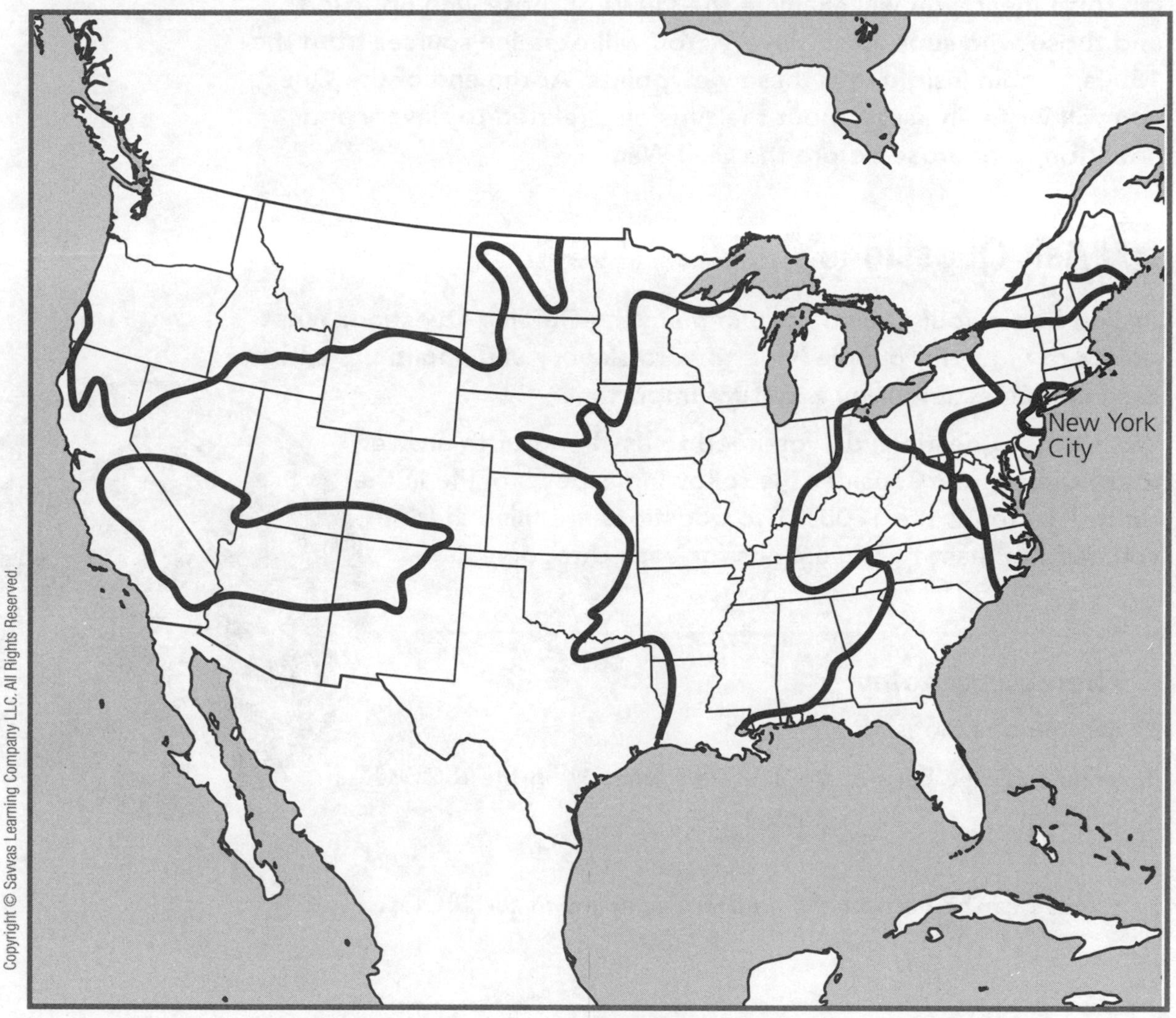

1840 1850 1860 1880

Slavery and Abolition

On this Quest, you will examine the views of those who opposed and those who supported slavery. You will examine sources from the 1800s to gain insight into these viewpoints. At the end of the Quest, you will write an essay about the tensions, related to slavery and abolition, that arose before the Civil War.

1 Ask Questions (See Student Text, page 318)

As you begin your Quest, keep in mind the Guiding Question: **What points of view did people have toward slavery and abolition?** and the Essential Question: **Why is culture important?**

What other questions do you need to ask in order to answer these questions? Consider the following aspects of life in the United States in the 1800s. Two questions are filled in for you. Add at least two questions for each category.

Theme Economy

Sample questions:

What was the basis of the southern economy in the 1800s?

What was the basis of the northern economy in the 1800s?

Theme Culture

Theme History

Theme New Inventions and Technology

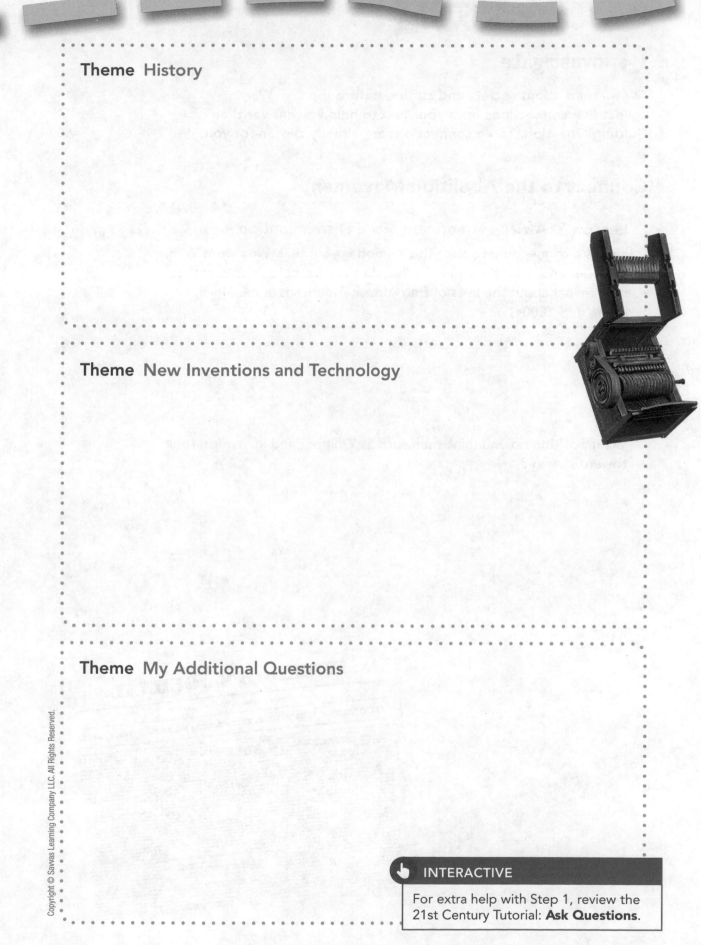

Theme My Additional Questions

INTERACTIVE

For extra help with Step 1, review the 21st Century Tutorial: **Ask Questions**.

2 Investigate

As you read about society and culture before the Civil War, collect five connections from your text to help you answer the Guiding Question. Three connections are already chosen for you.

Connect to the Abolition Movement

Lesson 2 African Americans Face Discrimination (See Student Text, page 339)

Here's a connection! Look at this section in your text. Who were William Whipper and John Russwurm? What do the accomplishments of these men reveal about the lives of free African Americans in the North in the mid-1800s?

What position do you think men such as Whipper and Russwurm took toward slavery?

FREEDOM'S JOURNAL.

"RIGHTEOUSNESS EXALTETH A NATION."

CORNISH & RUSSWURM, Editors and Proprietors.

NEW-YORK, FRIDAY, JUNE 22, 1827.

VOL. I, NO. 16.

Connect to the South's Economic Dependence

Lesson 3 Reliance on Plantation Agriculture (See Student Text, page 345)

Here's another connection! What does this section of the text tell you about the interaction between the southern and northern economies? On what was the southern economy based?

How might this situation have influenced the South's views on slavery?

Connect to Opponents of Slavery

Lesson 4 How Did Abolitionism Gain Momentum? (See Student Text, page 355)

What does this connection tell you about the two groups of people who opposed slavery?

What clue can you find in this section about how the abolitionists were received by those who supported slavery?

It's Your Turn! Find two more connections. Fill in the title of your connections, then answer the questions. Connections may be images, primary sources, maps, or text.

Your Choice | Connect to

Location in text

What is the main idea of this connection?

What does it tell you about the differing viewpoints in the United States toward slavery and abolition?

Your Choice | Connect to

Location in text

What is the main idea of this connection?

What does it tell you about the differing viewpoints in the United States toward slavery and abolition?

3 Examine Primary Sources (See Student Text, page 382)

Examine the primary and secondary sources provided online or from your teacher. Fill in the chart to show how these sources demonstrate points of view on both sides of the slavery issue. The first one is completed for you.

Source	Point of View
British Anti-Slavery Society Medallion, 1795	Abolition/Anti-slavery
"No Compromise With the Evil of Slavery"	
"Inhumanity of Slavery"	
The Southern Address of 1849	
1837 Broadside	
Cannibals All! Or, Slaves Without Masters	

INTERACTIVE

For extra help with Step 3, review the 21st Century Tutorials: **Analyze Primary and Secondary Sources** and **Compare and Contrast**.

4 Write Your Essay (See Student Text, page 382)

Now it's time to put together all of the information you have gathered and use it to write your essay.

1. **Prepare to Write** You have collected connections and explored primary and secondary sources that show the conflicting points of view about slavery held by Americans in the 1800s. Look through your notes and summarize these viewpoints. Record them here.

Viewpoints on Slavery and Abolition

2. **Write a Draft** Using evidence from the clues you found and the documents you explored, write a draft of your essay. Introduce the various viewpoints you have identified, then describe the cultural differences and personal attitudes behind them. Be sure to use vivid details that spring from evidence in the documents you've studied in this Quest.

3. **Share with a Partner** Exchange your draft with a partner. Tell your partner what you like about his or her draft and suggest any improvements.

4. **Finalize Your Essay** Revise your essay. Correct any grammatical or spelling errors. Be sure you have clearly described what you learned from the documents and how you used evidence from them to support your main points.

5. **Reflect on the Quest** Think about your experience completing this topic's Quest. What did you learn about the differing viewpoints on slavery and abolition? What questions do you still have about these views? How will you answer them?

Reflections

INTERACTIVE

For extra help with Step 4, review the 21st Century Tutorial: **Write an Essay**.

Take Notes

Literacy Skills: Cite Evidence Use what you have read to complete the table. In the first column, write one conclusion from the text. In the second column, write any evidence you can find in the text that supports this conclusion. The first one has been completed for you.

Conclusions	Evidence
New machines transformed the textile industry in England.	• In 1764, James Hargreaves developed the spinning jenny, allowing workers to spin several threads at once. • In the 1780s, Edmund Cartwright built a loom powered by water that allowed a worker to produce a great deal more cloth in a day than was possible before.

INTERACTIVE

For extra help, review the 21st Century Tutorial: **Support Ideas with Evidence**.

Practice Vocabulary

True or False? Decide whether each statement below is true or false. Circle T or F, and then explain your answer. Be sure to include the underlined vocabulary word in your explanation. The first one is done for you.

1. **T / F** The Industrial Revolution was a fight between factory workers and wealthy factory owners.
   False; The Industrial Revolution was a long, slow process that completely changed the way goods were produced and where people lived and worked.

2. **T / F** Setting up a new business requires capital, or money for investment.

3. **T / F** A capitalist is a person who is trained to use new technologies, such as the spinning jenny and water-powered loom.

4. **T / F** When factories cannot get enough raw materials, the supply of goods drops. Supply is the amount of goods available to sell.

5. **T / F** A large amount of goods, known as scarcity, causes prices to rise.

6. **T / F** Eli Whitney's idea of interchangeable parts meant that the parts of an object could be sold for a low price.

7. **T / F** The young women from nearby farms who came to work in the Lowell mills came to be called the Lowell girls.

8. **T / F** As industry grew, many people left farms for work in city factories, causing less urbanization.

Take Notes

Literacy Skills: Identify Main Ideas Use what you have read to complete the table. Use the details to identify the main idea. The first one has been completed for you.

What Changes Did the Age of Steam Power Bring?	How Did Workers Respond to Challenges?	How Did Ethnic Minorities Fare in the North?
Main Idea: The harnessing of steam power transformed many aspects of life in the United States. **Details:** Rail lines spread across the country. Factories also began to use steam, resulting in the expansion of industry and more affordable goods. Industrialization improved the standard of living.	**Main Idea:** **Details:**	**Main Idea:** **Details:**

A Reaction Against Immigrants	African Americans Face Discrimination
Main Idea: **Details:**	**Main Idea:** **Details:**

INTERACTIVE

For extra help, review the 21st Century Tutorial: **Identify Main Ideas and Details.**

Practice Vocabulary

Vocabulary Quiz Show Some quiz shows ask a question and expect the contestant to give the answer. In other shows, the contestant is given an answer and must supply the question. If the blank is in the Question column, write the question that would result in the answer in the Answer column. If the question is supplied, write the answer.

Question	Answer
1. What is another term for a skilled worker?	1.
2.	2. famine
3.	3. discrimination
4. What action, in which workers refused to do their jobs until their demands were met, was illegal in many parts of the country in the early 1800s?	4.
5.	5. Know-Nothing Party
6.	6. nativists
7. What groups were formed when artisans united to protest poor working conditions and low wages?	7.

Take Notes

Literacy Skills: Compare and Contrast Use what you have read to complete the charts comparing and contrasting aspects of life in the South. The first one has been completed for you.

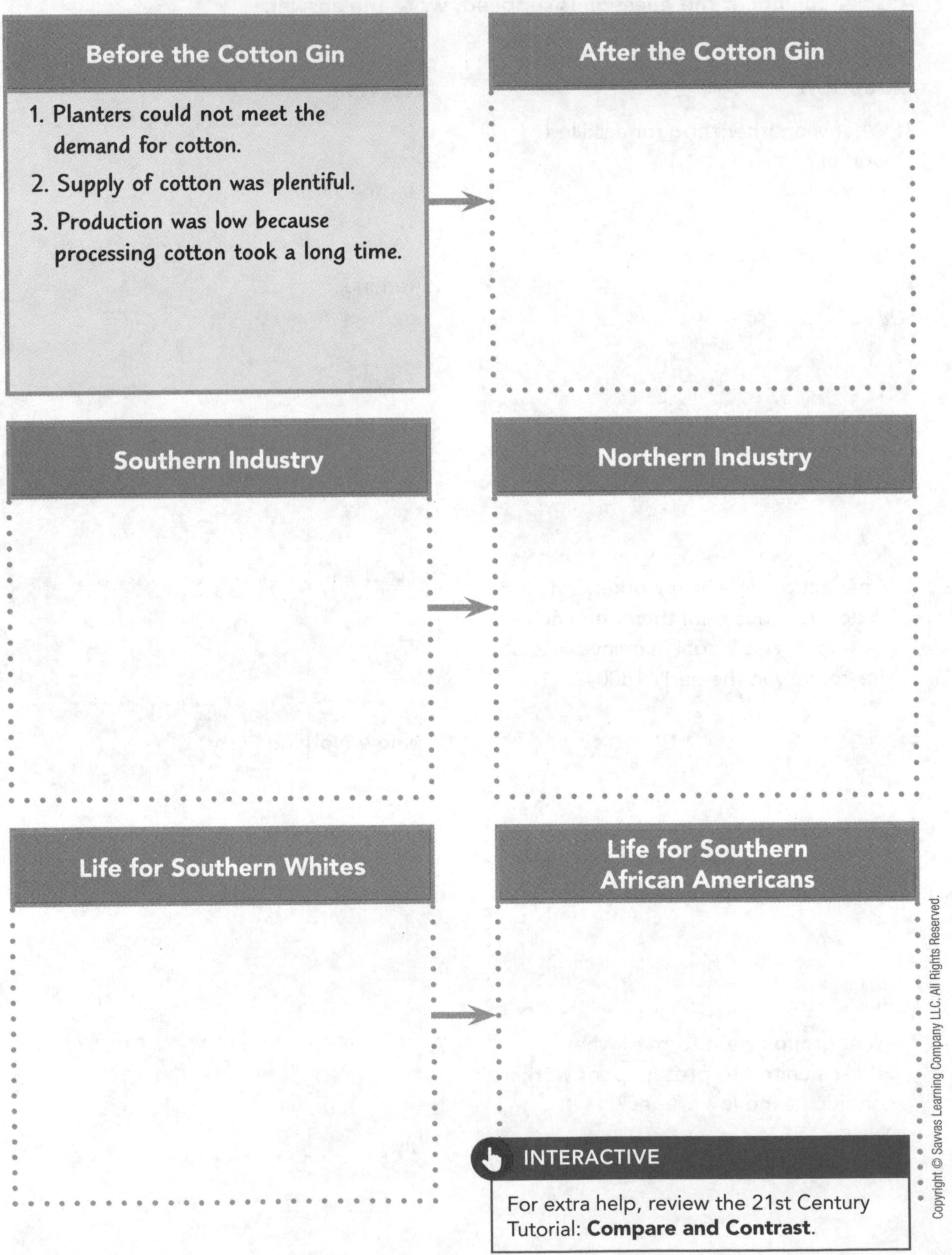

Before the Cotton Gin
1. Planters could not meet the demand for cotton.
2. Supply of cotton was plentiful.
3. Production was low because processing cotton took a long time.
After the Cotton Gin
Southern Industry
Northern Industry
Life for Southern Whites
Life for Southern African Americans

INTERACTIVE

For extra help, review the 21st Century Tutorial: **Compare and Contrast**.

Practice Vocabulary

Matching Logic **Using your knowledge of the underlined vocabulary words, draw a line from each sentence in Column 1 to match it with the sentence in Column 2 to which it logically belongs.**

Column 1	Column 2
1. The views and way of life of the "cottonocracy" dominated the South.	Before planting, farmers must prepare the land.
2. This idea of the extended family had its roots in Africa.	Swift growth in cotton production meant that by 1850, planters were producing more than 2 million bales of cotton a year.
3. Under the slave codes, enslaved African Americans could not leave their owner's land without a written pass.	These wealthy planter families lived mainly in the cotton belt of the lowland South and in coastal areas of South Carolina, Georgia, and Louisiana.
4. The invention of the cotton gin meant that planters needed more land to cultivate.	They were designed to keep enslaved African Americans from running away or rebelling.
5. Slavery spread as a result of the cotton boom.	Grandparents, parents, children, aunts, uncles, and cousins formed a close-knit group.

Take Notes

Literacy Skills: Summarize Use what you have read to complete the table. In each space, write an important point related to that topic. Then summarize the lesson. The first one has been completed for you.

What Form Did Early Opposition to Slavery Take?	How Did Abolitionism Gain Momentum?	Who Opposed the Abolitionists?
Slavery in the 1800s Slavery was gradually ended in the North; religious beliefs led some to oppose slavery; slavery was banned in the Northwest Territory.	**Abolitionists**	**Northerners Against Abolition**
The Colonization Movement The American Colonization Society proposed to end slavery by setting up an independent colony in Africa for Africans and African Americans.	**Civil Disobedience and the Underground Railroad** ***Uncle Tom's Cabin***	**Southerners Defend Slavery Against the North**

Summary:

INTERACTIVE

For extra help, review the 21st Century Tutorial: **Summarize**.

Practice Vocabulary

Sentence Builder **Finish the sentences below with a vocabulary term from this section. You may have to change the form of the words to complete the sentences.**

Word Bank

American Colonization Society
abolitionist
The Liberator
Underground Railroad
civil disobedience

1. A person who wanted to end slavery in the United States was known as a(n)

2. "Conductors" guided runaways to "stations" where they could spend the night on the

3. Disobeying laws that one feels are unjust is known as

4. The group that President Monroe helped to set up a colony in western Africa was called the

5. William Lloyd Garrison called his antislavery newspaper

Quick Activity Abolitionists Speak Out

With a partner or small group, examine this 1859 flyer announcing the sale of enslaved people.

NEGROES

FOR SALE.

I will sell by Public Auction, on Tuesday of next Court, being the 29th of November, *Eight Valuable Family Servants*, consisting of one Negro Man, a first-rate field hand, one No. 1 Boy, 17 years o' age, a trusty house servant, one excellent Cook, one House-Maid, and one Seamstress. The balance are under 12 years of age. They are sold for no fault, but in consequence of my going to reside North. Also a quantity of Household and Kitchen Furniture, Stable Lot, &c. Terms accommodating, and made known on day of sale.

Jacob August.

P. J. TURNBULL, *Auctioneer.*

***Warrenton, October* 28, 1859.**

Printed at the *News* office, Warrenton, North Carolina.

How might an abolitionist use the information in this flyer to point out some of the evils of slavery? Refer to specific parts of the flyer in your answer.

> *We* do not preach rebellion—no, but submission and peace. Our enemies may accuse us of striving to stir up the slaves to revenge but their accusations are false, and made only to excite the prejudices of the whites, and to destroy our influence. We say, that the possibility of a bloody insurrection at the south fills us with dismay; and we avow, too, as plainly, that if any people were ever justified in throwing off the yoke of their tyrants, the slaves are that people. It is not we, but our guilty countrymen, who put arguments into the mouths, and swords into the hands of the slaves. Every sentence that they write—every word that they speak—every resistance that they make, against foreign oppression, is a call upon their slaves to destroy them. Every Fourth of July celebration must embitter and inflame the minds of the slaves.
>
> — William Lloyd Garrison, Editorial, *The Liberator* (January 8, 1831)

Team Challenge! **The excerpt above is from an 1831 editorial. An editorial is a newspaper article that gives an opinion on a particular issue. Work with your group to write an editorial about the work of abolitionists that might have appeared in your local newspaper in the 1850s. Find an image from your text or online that you might use to illustrate the editorial, then design the article and illustration to look like a real page from a newspaper.**

Take Notes

Literacy Skills: Draw Conclusions Use what you have read to complete the table. In the right column, write conclusions that can be drawn from the information in the box to the left. The first one has been completed for you.

Main Idea	Conclusion
Reformers fought to end slavery, increase access to education, improve conditions in prisons, expand women's rights, and more.	Conflict likely erupted between reformers and those who wanted things to stay as they were.
Women often played a leading role in reform movements.	
By the 1850s, most northern states had set up free tax-supported elementary schools.	
Women had few legal or political rights at this time.	
The *Declaration of Sentiments* was modeled on the Declaration of Independence.	
Women won new opportunities in education and employment.	

INTERACTIVE

For extra help, review the 21st Century Tutorial: **Draw Conclusions**.

Practice Vocabulary

Use a Word Bank **Choose one word from the word bank to fill in each blank. When you have finished, you will have a short summary of important ideas from the section.**

Word Bank

social reform	women's rights movement
debtors	temperance movement
Seneca Falls Convention	Second Great Awakening

Some Americans saw many things that needed to be fixed during the Era of Reform. Dorothea Dix convinced state prison systems to stop cruel punishment and the treatment of __________ as criminals. Those who took part in the __________ urged people to drink less alcohol or stop drinking altogether. Much of the impulse toward __________ at this time had its roots in the __________ that swept the nation. This movement taught that people could save their souls by their actions. Inspired by religion and their work on other causes, women met at the __________ in 1848 to discuss equal rights for women. This meeting was the beginning of the long- and still-continuing __________.

Quick Activity An Echo Across Time

In 1776, the founders of the United States declared their independence from Britain with these ringing words:

> . . . The history of the present King of Great Britain is a history of repeated injuries and usurpations, all having in direct object the establishment of an absolute Tyranny over these States. To prove this, let Facts be submitted to a candid world.
>
> He has refused his Assent to Laws, the most wholesome and necessary for the public good.
>
> He has forbidden his Governors to pass Laws of immediate and pressing importance.
>
> —The Declaration of Independence (1776)

More than seventy years later, the women who attended the Seneca Falls Convention declared their own independence. Underline words and phrases that are the same in the two declarations.

> The history of mankind is a history of repeated injuries and usurpations on the part of man toward woman, having in direct object the establishment of an absolute tyranny over her. To prove this, let facts be submitted to a candid world.
>
> He has never permitted her to exercise her inalienable right to the elective franchise.
>
> He has compelled her to submit to laws, in the formation of which she had no voice.
>
> —*The Declaration of Sentiments and Resolutions, 1848*

Team Challenge! With a partner or small group, explore the similarities between the Declaration of Independence and the Declaration of Sentiments. Then answer this question: Why do you think the writers of the Declaration of Sentiments chose to model their work on the earlier document?

Take Notes

Literacy Skills: Identify Cause and Effect Use what you have read to complete the diagrams. Two causes have been completed for you.

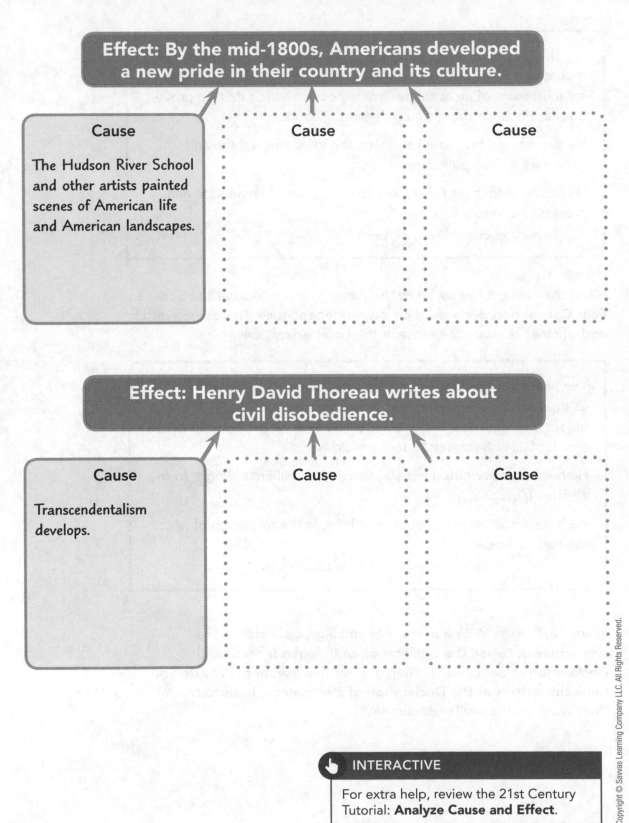

Effect: By the mid-1800s, Americans developed a new pride in their country and its culture.

Cause	Cause	Cause
The Hudson River School and other artists painted scenes of American life and American landscapes.		

Effect: Henry David Thoreau writes about civil disobedience.

Cause	Cause	Cause
Transcendentalism develops.		

INTERACTIVE

For extra help, review the 21st Century Tutorial: **Analyze Cause and Effect.**

Practice Vocabulary

Word Map **Study the word map for the term *Hudson River School.* Characteristics are words or phrases that relate to the term in the center of the word map. Non-characteristics are words and phrases not associated with that term. Use the blank word map to explore the meaning of the word *transcendentalist.* Then make a word map of your own for the word *individualism.***

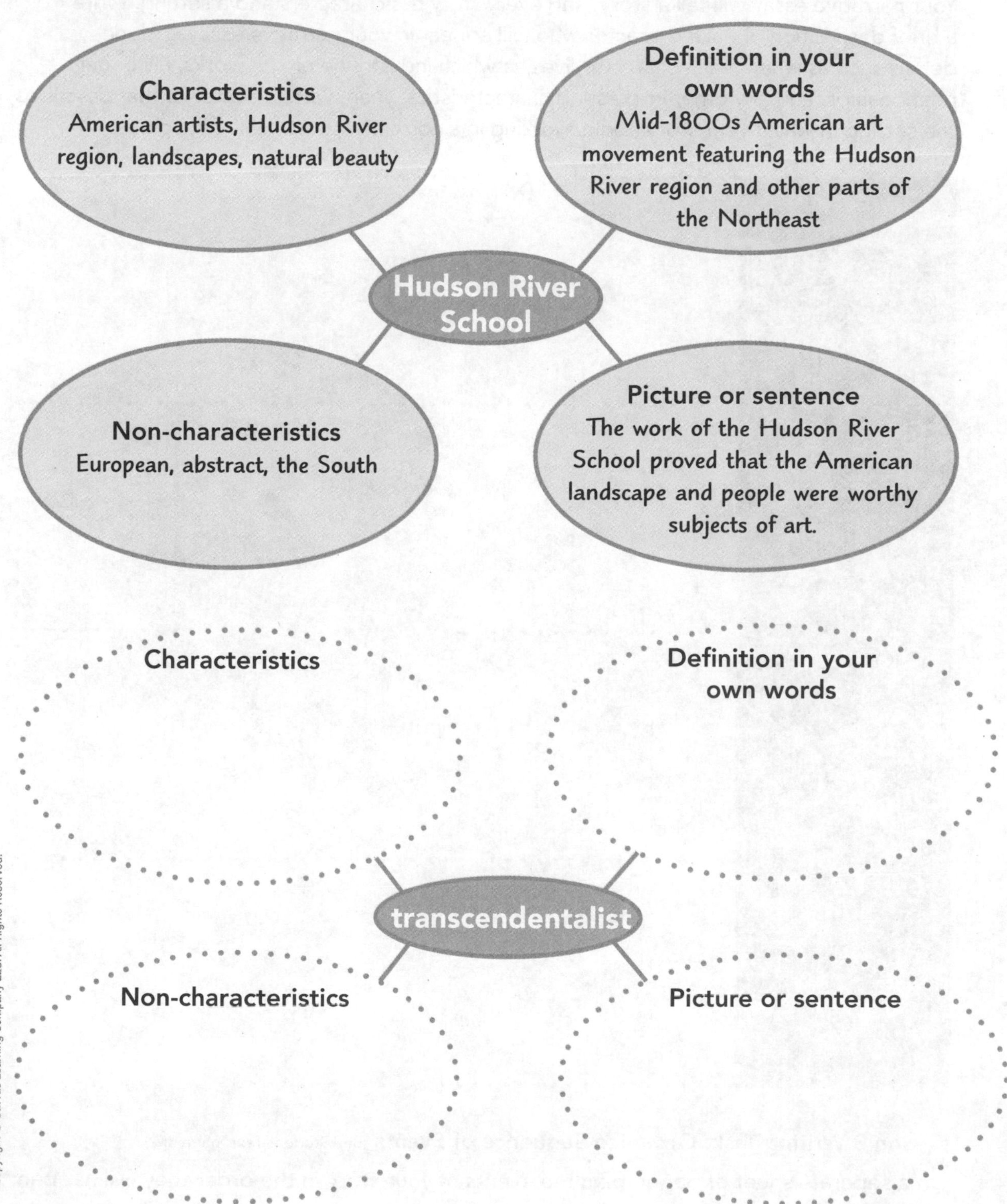

Characteristics
American artists, Hudson River region, landscapes, natural beauty
Definition in your own words
Mid-1800s American art movement featuring the Hudson River region and other parts of the Northeast
Hudson River School
Non-characteristics
European, abstract, the South
Picture or sentence
The work of the Hudson River School proved that the American landscape and people were worthy subjects of art.
Characteristics
Definition in your own words
transcendentalist
Non-characteristics
Picture or sentence

Writing Workshop Narrative Essay

As you read, build a response to this topic: Write a three-paragraph narrative essay from the point of view of a young person working in northern industry during this time period. The prompts below will help walk you through the process.

Lessons 1 and 2 Writing Tasks: Introduce Characters and Establish Setting

(See Student Text, pages 330 and 340)

Your narrative essay will tell a story, and every story has characters and a setting. Write a brief description of each character who will appear in your narrative essay. Include details such as where each character lives, in which industry he or she works, his or her relationships, and any other interesting characteristics. Then, write a sentence that describes the setting in which your story about working in a northern industry will take place.

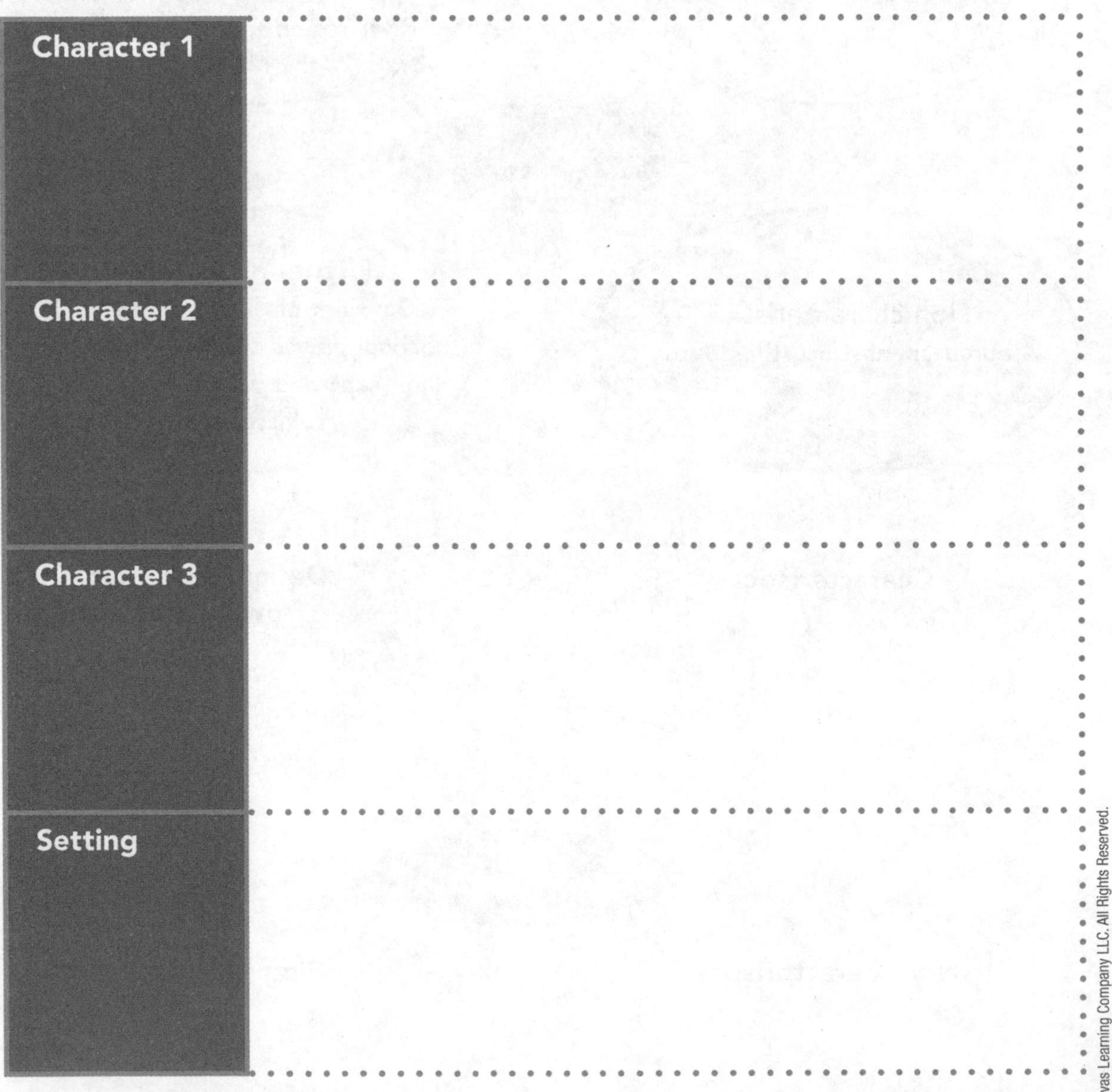

Lesson 3 Writing Task: Organize Sequence of Events (See Student Text, page 352)

On a separate sheet of paper, plan the events of your story in the order they will happen.

Lessons 4 and 5 Writing Tasks: Use Narrative Techniques, Descriptive Details, and Sensory Language (See Student Text, pages 359 and 373)

Will you tell your story using the first person point of view—"I lived . . ." or "I saw . . ."? Or the third person—"He lived . . ." or "He saw . . ."? Will you use present or past tense? Will you include dialogue? After deciding these points, think about how to bring your story to life. Write some descriptive words and sensory language about where you are sitting right now. Then, write descriptive words and sensory language related to your story.

What point of view?	
What tense?	
Dialogue?	
Descriptive words/ sensory language: My setting	
Descriptive words/ sensory language: My story	

Lesson 6 Writing Task: Prepare a Final Draft (See Student Text, page 381)

Using the details you have fleshed out here, write a first draft of your story. After you have finished, review your work. Check your structure, spelling, and grammar, and prepare a final draft.

Writing Task (See Student Text, page 383)

Read your final draft. Does the story follow the plan you set out here? Does it accurately describe life for a young person working in a northern industry during the Industrial Revolution? Once you are satisfied with your work, trade essays with a partner. Make any corrections or improvements your partner suggests.

Sectionalism and Civil War Preview

Essential Question When is war justified?

Before you begin this topic, think about the Essential Question by completing the following activity.

1. What factors justify going to war? Read the list below, then write a paragraph explaining which of these factors would justify going to war and which would not.

economic factors	religious factors
political factors	social factors

Timeline Skills

As you read, write and/or draw at least three events from the topic. Draw a line from each event to its correct position on the timeline.

1820	1830	1840

Map Skills

Using maps throughout the topic, add the state abbreviations for those states that are missing labels. Then use different colors to shade the Union states, the Border states, the Confederate states, and the territories.

California	Georgia	Kansas	Kentucky
Mississippi	New York	Ohio	South Carolina
Texas	Virginia	West Virginia	

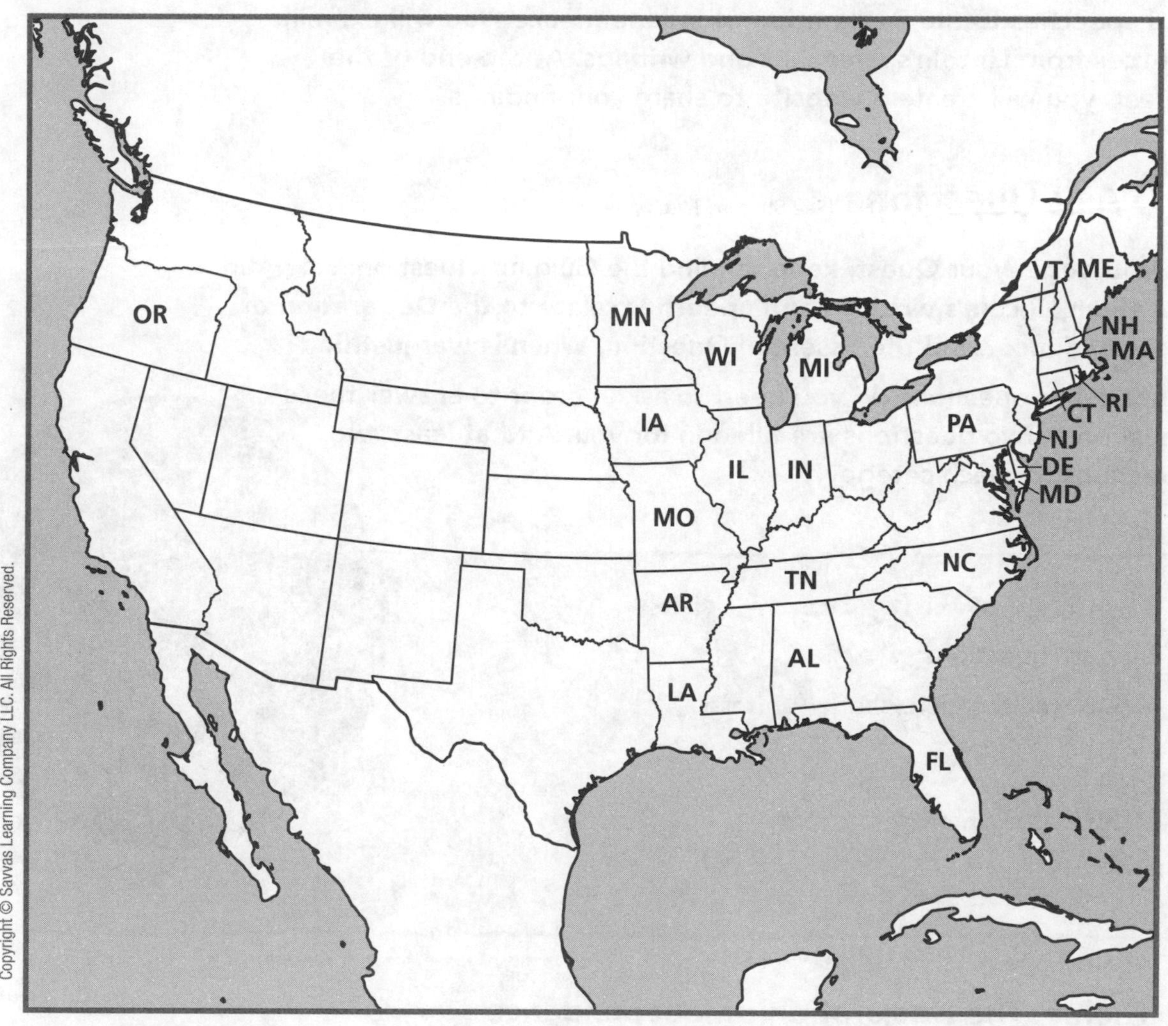

1850 1860 1870

A Lincoln Website

On this Quest, you need to compare Abraham Lincoln's writings and speeches to the Declaration of Independence. You will examine sources from Lincoln's speeches and writings. At the end of the Quest, you will create a website to share your findings.

1 Ask Questions (See Student Text, page 388)

As you begin your Quest, keep in mind the Guiding Question: **How did Abraham Lincoln's writings and speeches relate to the Declaration of Independence?** and the Essential Question: **When is war justified?**

What other questions do you need to ask in order to answer these questions? Two questions are filled in for you. Add at least two questions for each category.

Theme The Gettysburg Address

Sample questions:

What was the Gettysburg Address?

Why is it memorable?

Theme The Declaration of Independence

Theme Preserving the Union

Theme Election of 1864

Theme My Additional Questions

INTERACTIVE

For extra help with Step 1, review the 21st Century Tutorial: **Ask Questions**.

Quest CONNECTIONS

2 Investigate

As you read about President Lincoln and the Civil War, collect five connections from your text to help you answer the Guiding Question. Three connections are already chosen for you.

Connect to the Lincoln/Douglas Debates

Lesson 2 How Did Abraham Lincoln Come to Lead the Republican Party? (See Student Text, page 407)

Here's a connection! Find the passage in the Declaration of Independence that explains the rights that all men should have. How do Lincoln's comments during his series of debates with Stephen Douglas support the ideas expressed in the Declaration of Independence?

What were Stephen Douglas's views on popular sovereignty? What were Lincoln's views?

Connect to the Right to Alter or to Abolish

Lesson 3 A Move Toward Civil War (See Student Text, page 413)

Here's another connection! What does the Declaration of Independence say about the people's displeasure with their current government?

Secessionists leaving the Union.

What does Lincoln say about this in his speeches?

Connect to the Emancipation Proclamation

Primary Source Abraham Lincoln, The Emancipation Proclamation

(See Student Text, page 441)

What does the Declaration of Independence say about the responsibility of government to protect the safety and happiness of the people?

How is this passage in the Declaration of Independence reflected in the Emancipation Proclamation?

It's Your Turn! Find two more connections. Fill in the title of your connections, then answer the questions. Connections may be images, primary sources, maps, or text.

Your Choice | Connect to

Location in text

What is the main idea of this connection?

What does it tell you about Lincoln's understanding of the Declaration of Independence?

Your Choice | Connect to

Location in text

What is the main idea of this connection?

What does it tell you about Lincoln's understanding of the Declaration of Independence?

3 Conduct Research (See Student Text, page 454)

Examine Abraham Lincoln's Emancipation Proclamation in your text. Then find additional writings and speeches from Lincoln in the text or online. List these additional sources in the chart and then note how they reveal the ways that Lincoln's speeches and writings relate to the Declaration of Independence. The first one is completed for you.

Abraham Lincoln's Writings/Speeches	Relation to the Declaration of Independence
Emancipation Proclamation (1863)	"All men are created equal," including enslaved people. Government is responsible for protecting the rights of all people, including the enslaved.

INTERACTIVE

For extra help with Step 3, review the 21st Century Tutorial: **Analyze Primary and Secondary Sources**.

4 Create a Website (See Student Text, page 454)

Now is the time to put together all of the information you have gathered and use it to create your two-page website. Work with a partner or team. Familiarize yourself with digital tools and software to help you create images and text for your website.

1. **Prepare to Write** You have collected connections and explored primary sources that show how Lincoln's speeches and writings reflected ideas in the Declaration of Independence. Look through your notes and decide which speeches and writings you want to highlight on your website. Record them here. Then, decide which team member will write and design each section of your website.

Lincoln's Writings and Speeches

2. **Write a Draft** Using evidence from the clues you found and the documents you explored, write a draft of your section of the website, including any visuals you plan to use.

3. **Share with a Partner** Exchange your draft with a partner. Tell your partner what you like about his or her draft and suggest any improvements.

4. **Finalize Your Plans for Your Website.** Make any revisions needed. Are your explanations clear? Do your images relate well to your content? Once you finalize your plans, create your website.

5. **Reflect on the Quest** Think about your experience completing this topic's Quest. What did you learn about Abraham Lincoln and his admiration for the ideas in the Declaration of Independence? What questions do you still have about his writings and how they reflect ideas in the Declaration of Independence? How will you answer them?

Reflections

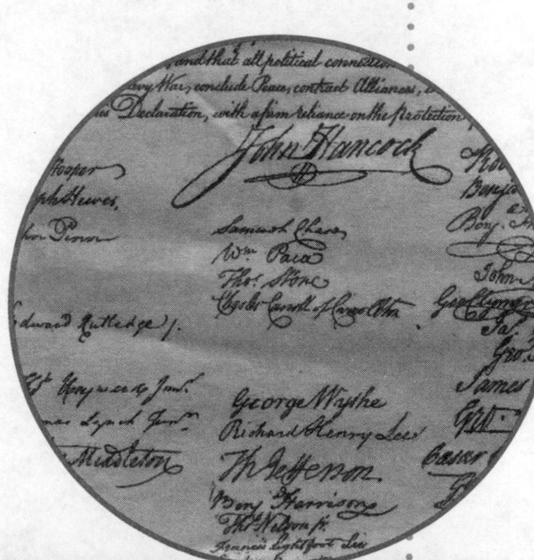

INTERACTIVE

For extra help with Step 4, review the 21st Century Tutorial: **Evaluate Web Sites**.

Take Notes

Literacy Skills: Compare and Contrast Use what you have learned to complete the Venn diagram. Compare and contrast the Missouri Compromise of 1820 and the Missouri Compromise of 1850. In what ways were the provisions different? In what ways were the provisions the same? The first entry has been completed for you.

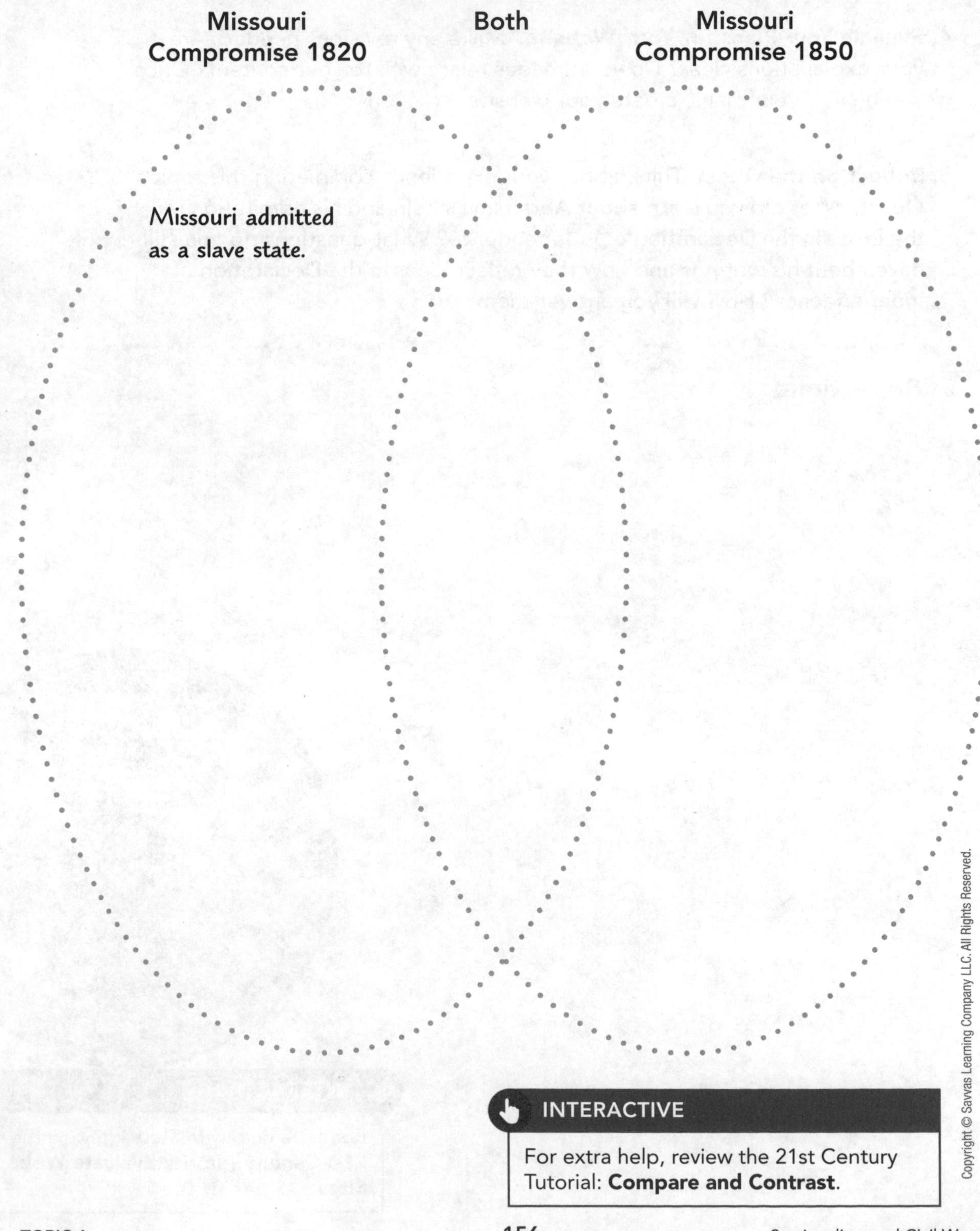

INTERACTIVE

For extra help, review the 21st Century Tutorial: **Compare and Contrast**.

Practice Vocabulary

True or False? Decide whether each statement below is true or false. Circle T or F, and then explain your answer. Be sure to include the underlined vocabulary word in your explanation. The first one is done for you.

1. **T / F** The Missouri Compromise was a series of laws in 1820 that favored the admission of free states to the Union.
   False; The Missouri Compromise was a series of laws in 1820 and 1850 that maintained a balance between free and slave states admitted to the Union.

2. **T / F** The newly formed Free-Soil Party, whose members were mostly southerners, campaigned for popular sovereignty in the western territories.

3. **T / F** Southerners felt justified in the decision to secede because they said the North did not respect the compact between states as set forth in the Constitution.

4. **T / F** Bleeding Kansas was the result of the repeal of popular sovereignty in Kansas and Nebraska.

5. **T / F** The Compromise of 1850 applied to the Louisiana Purchase and the Mexican Cession.

6. **T / F** The Fugitive Slave Act of 1850, with added provisions and heavier punishments, was more harsh than the Fugitive Slave Act passed in 1793.

7. **T / F** Daniel Webster felt the Compromise of 1850 would not prevent civil war.

8. **T / F** Personal liberty laws passed in the North allowed fugitives to argue their cases before a court.

Take Notes

Literacy Skills: Identify Cause and Effect Use what you have learned to complete the chart. Write the effects of each event on the North and on the South. The first one is completed for you.

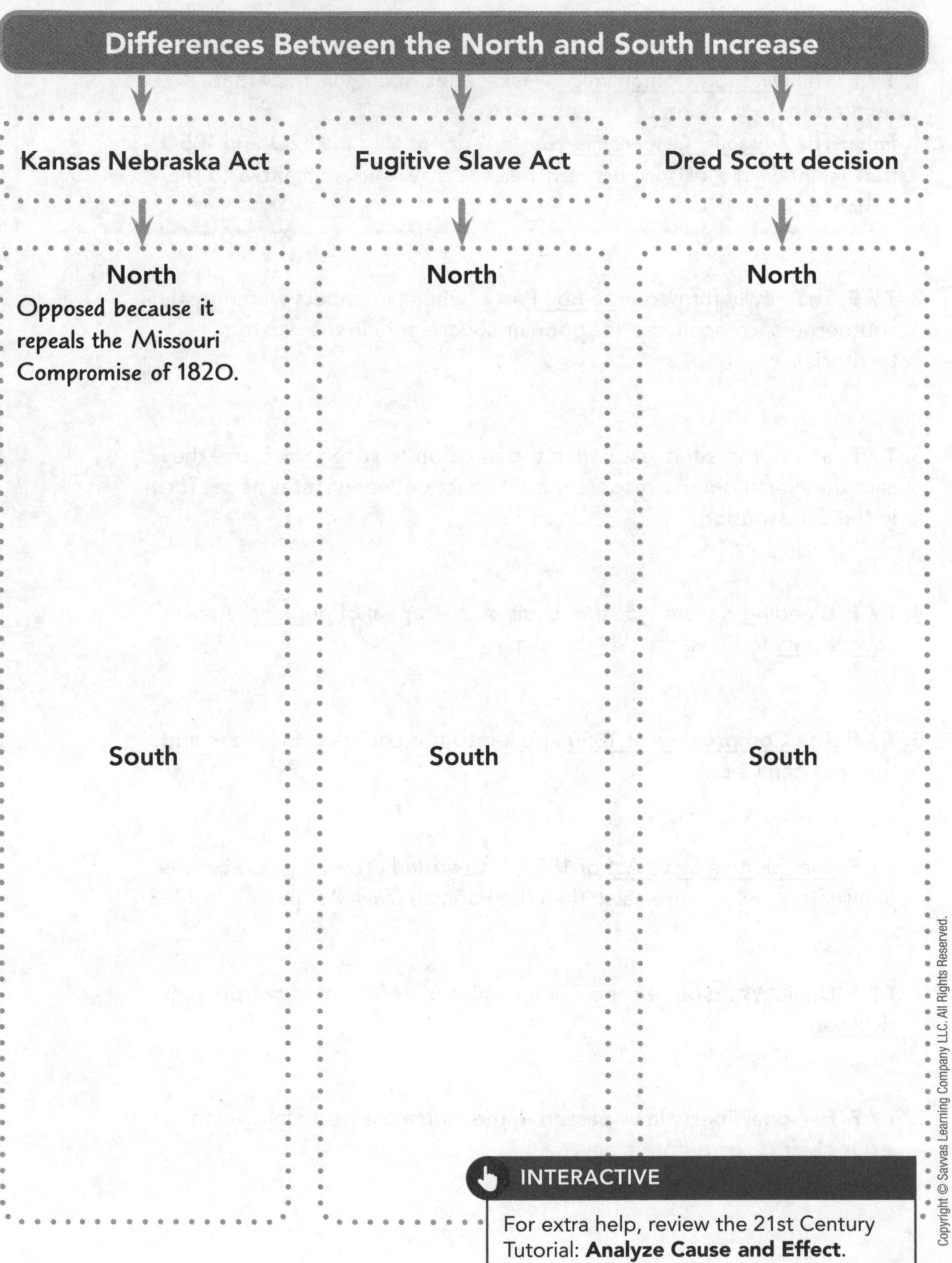

Differences Between the North and South Increase
Kansas Nebraska Act
Fugitive Slave Act
Dred Scott decision
North
Opposed because it repeals the Missouri Compromise of 1820.
North
North
South
South
South

INTERACTIVE

For extra help, review the 21st Century Tutorial: **Analyze Cause and Effect.**

Practice Vocabulary

Vocabulary Quiz Show Some quiz shows ask a question and expect the contestant to give the answer. In other shows, the contestant is given an answer and must supply the question. If the blank is in the Question column, write the question that would result in the answer in the Answer column. If the question is supplied, write the answer.

Question	Answer
1.	1. martyr
2. What measure did Stephen Douglas propose to organize government in two territories?	2.
3.	3. arsenal
4. What said that Congress did not have the power to ban slavery in the territories?	4.
5. Which proslavery group traveled to the Kansas-Nebraska territory to set up a government?	5.
6.	6. treason
7. What organization attracted people who were opposed to the spread of slavery in the western territories?	7.
8. What is it called when informal military groups use hit-and-run tactics?	8.

Quick Activity Formerly a Slave

With a partner or small group, read the excerpt below. It is the narrative of an escaped slave, Nancy Howard. Her story is part of a collection of narratives of former slaves who escaped to Canada. The stories were gathered by Boston abolitionist Benjamin Drew.

> I was born in Arundel County, Maryland—was brought up in Baltimore. After my escape, I lived in Lynn, Mass., seven years. But I left there, through fear of being carried back, owing to the fugitive slave law. I have lived in St. Catherines [Ontario, Canada] less than a year.
>
> The way I got away was—my mistress was sick and went into the country for her health. I went to stay with her cousin. After a month, my mistress was sent back to the city to her cousin's and I waited on her. My daughter had been off [successfully escaped] three years. A friend said to me—"Now is your chance to get off." At last I concluded to go—the friend supplying me with money. I was asked no questions on the way north.
>
> —from Benjamin Drew, *The Refugee: Narratives of Fugitive Slaves in Canada Related by Themselves* (1856)

This is one story. Why did Nancy leave Massachusetts? Do you think her fears were justified? Explain your answer.

Team Challenge! The picture above shows African Americans arriving at a place where they can live in freedom. How do you think these people feel? If you were an enslaved person planning to escape, would your plans be influenced by the *Dred Scott* decision? Working with your partner or group, write a short narrative from the viewpoint of the enslaved person that tells whether or not you will keep your plans to escape in light of this decision. Share your stories with the class.

Take Notes

Literacy Skills: Compare and Contrast Use what you have read to complete the tables. List the differences between the North and South during the early years of the Civil War. The first entry is completed for you.

	North	South
Reason for fighting	• *To preserve the Union*	• *To preserve their way of life*
Advantages		
Disadvantages		

INTERACTIVE

For extra help, review the 21st Century Tutorial: **Compare and Contrast**.

Practice Vocabulary

Word Map Study the word map for the word *unamendable.* Characteristics are words or phrases that relate to the term in the center of the word map. Non-characteristics are words and phrases not associated with that term. Use the blank word map to explore the meaning of the word *acquiescence.* Then make a word map of your own for the term *border state.*

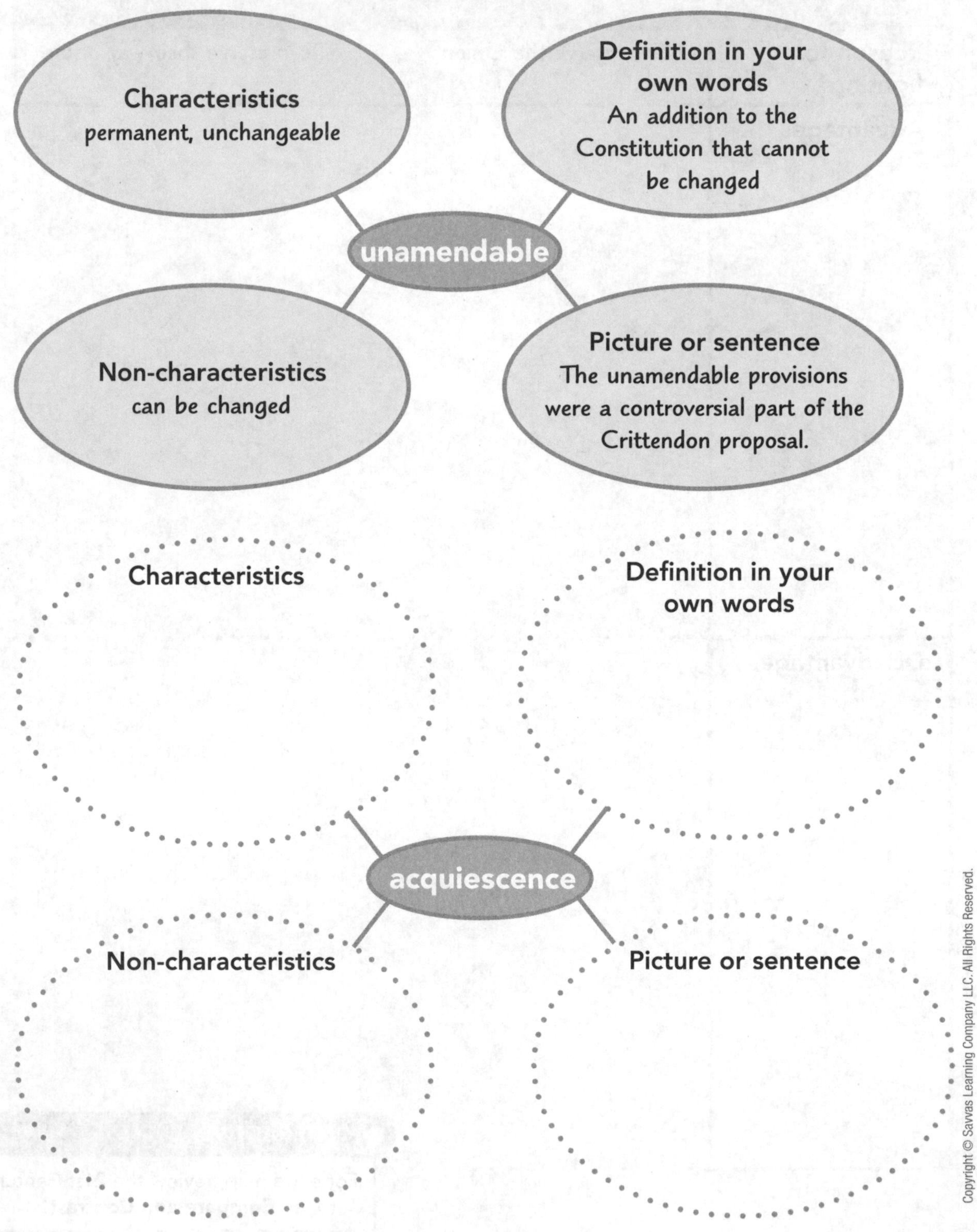

Take Notes

Literacy Skills: Sequence Use what you have read to complete the timeline with the five important battles that occurred during 1862. Then, in the box at bottom, write the significance of each battle.

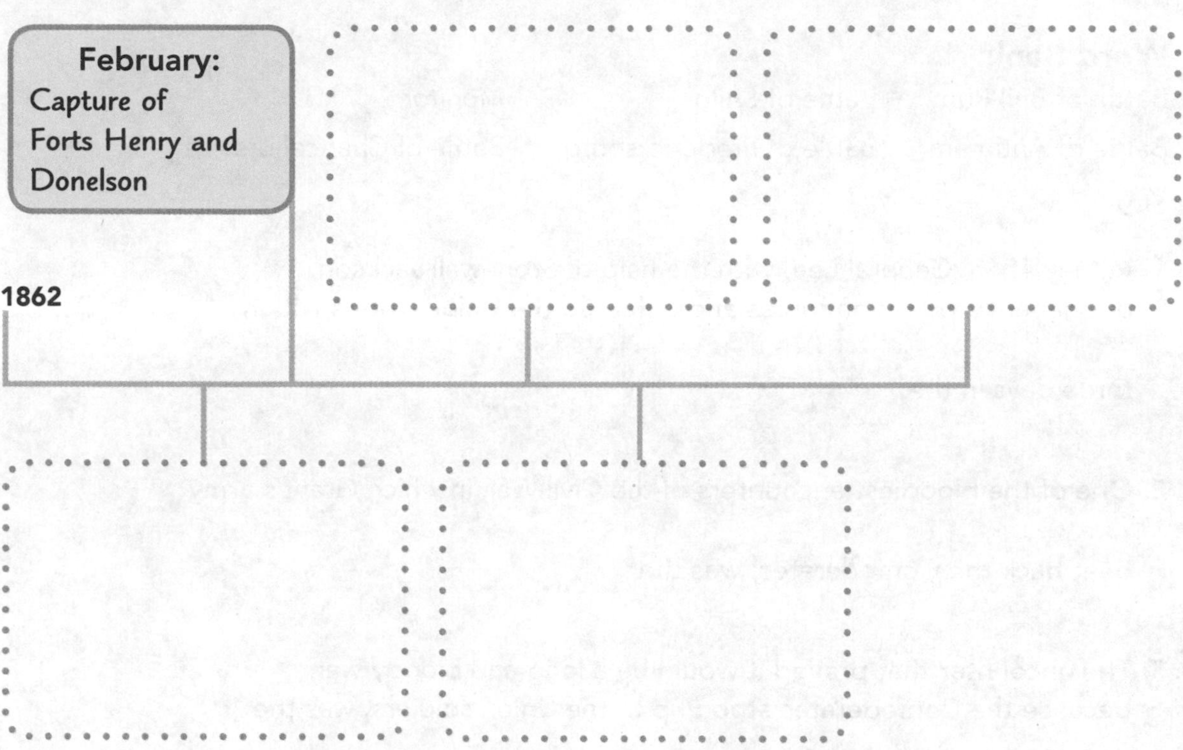

Significance of Battles

INTERACTIVE

For extra help, review the 21st Century Tutorial: **Sequence**.

Practice Vocabulary

Sentence Builder **Finish the sentences below with a key term from this section. You may have to change the form of the words to complete the sentences.**

Word Bank

Battle of Bull Run | Battle of Shiloh | *Monitor*
Battle of Antietam | Battle of Fredericksburg | Battle of Chancellorsville
Virginia

1. In May 1863, General Lee, with the help of Stonewall Jackson, outmaneuvered Union forces and defeated the Union troops within three days in the ____________.

2. One of the bloodiest encounters of the Civil War, in which Grant's army beat back the Confederates, was the ____________.

3. The encounter that proved it would be a long and bloody war, because the Confederates stood up to the Union soldiers, was the ____________.

4. The Confederates renamed the USS *Merrimack* warship to the ____________.

5. The battle that allowed the North to claim victory because General Lee withdrew his troops was the ____________.

6. After the Confederates took the *Virginia* out for battle, the Union countered with their own ironclad, called the ____________.

7. The encounter that was one of the Union's worst defeats, and resulted in Burnside being relieved of command, was the ____________.

Take Notes

Literacy Skills: Summarize Use what you have read to complete the chart. After you have completed the chart, provide a summary describing how these factors changed or challenged the North and South during the Civil War. The first entry Is completed for you.

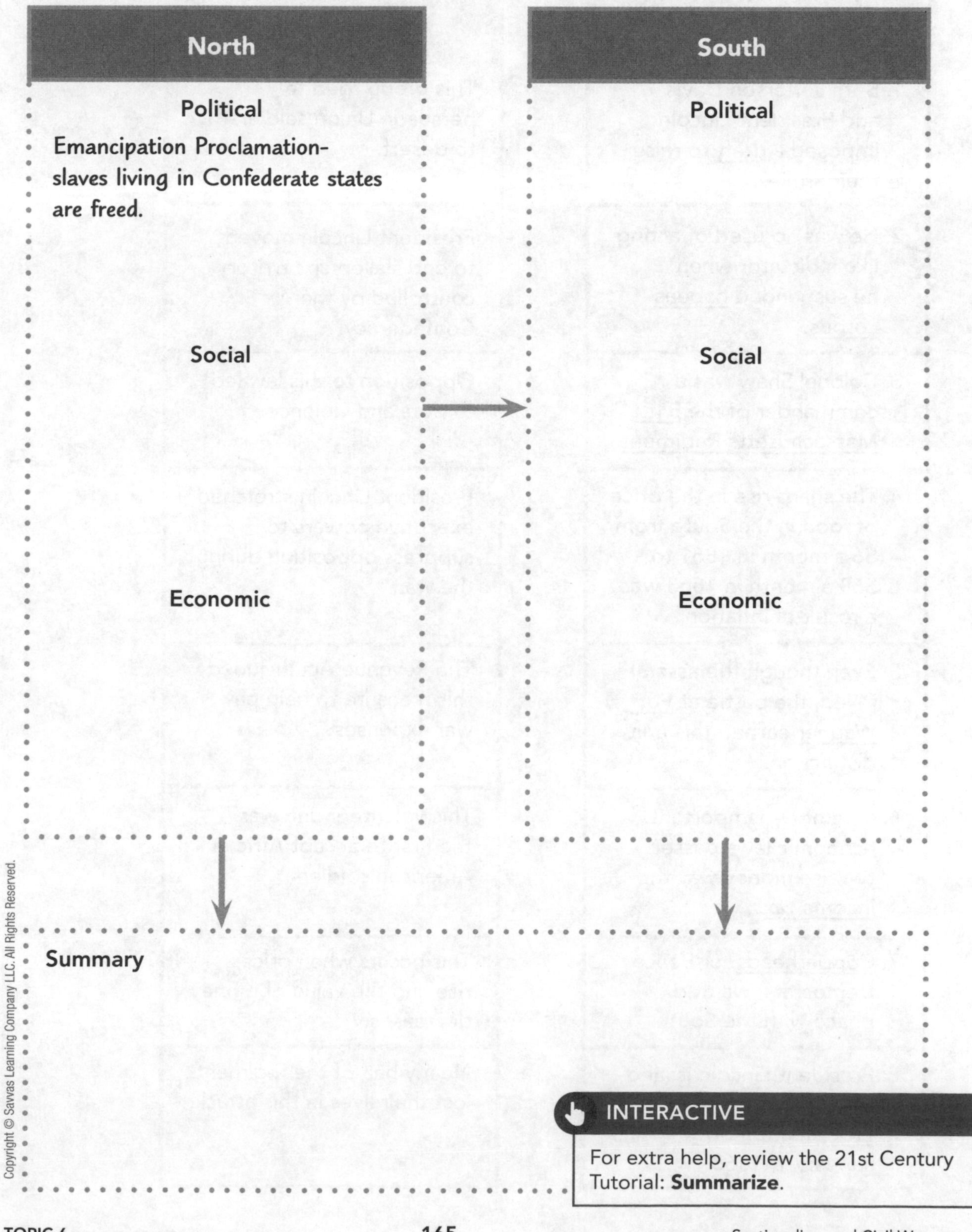

North	South
Political Emancipation Proclamation- slaves living in Confederate states are freed.	**Political**
Social	**Social**
Economic	**Economic**

Summary

INTERACTIVE

For extra help, review the 21st Century Tutorial: **Summarize**.

Practice Vocabulary

Matching Logic Using your knowledge of the underlined words, draw a line from each sentence in Column 1 to match it with the sentence in Column 2 to which it logically belongs.

Column 1	Column 2
1. Both Jefferson Davis and President Lincoln imposed a draft to raise their armies.	This group tried to persuade Union soldiers to desert.
2. He was accused of acting like a dictator when he suspended habeas corpus.	President Lincoln moved to end slavery in territory controlled by the Confederacy.
3. Colonel Shaw was a commander of the 54th Massachusetts Regiment.	Opposition to this law led to riots and violence.
4. The sharp rise in the price of food in the South from $6 a month in 1861 to $68 a month in 1863 was a result of inflation.	President Lincoln stretched executive powers to suppress opposition during the war.
5. Even though the assault failed, the battle at Fort Wagner earned this unit distinction.	The Revenue Act included this measure to help pay war expenses.
6. One of two important economic laws passed to raise money was the income tax.	This volunteer unit was the first to accept African American soldiers.
7. Copperheads, or Peace Democrats, wanted peace with the South.	This occurs when prices rise and the value of money decreases.
8. President Lincoln issued the Emancipation Proclamation on January 1, 1863.	Nearly half of the regiment lost their lives in this attack.

Quick Activity Living through the War

As the war moved into its third year, the effect on civilians became more difficult. The account below is from Agnes, who lived in Richmond, Virginia.

> The crowd now rapidly increased and numbered, I am sure more than a thousand women and children. It grew and grew until it reached the dignity of a mob—a bread riot.
>
> —Agnes, quoted in *Reminiscences of Peace and War*

While the account is brief, it still creates a picture in the reader's mind. Working with a partner or a small group, give a one-minute news report of the situation. What do you know about the crowd? What was the mood? Who was affected? Then read the accounts of a soldier's life during the war.

> The first thing in the morning is drill. Then drill, then drill again. Then drill, drill, a little more drill. Then drill and lastly drill.

> Look at our company—21 have died of disease, 18 have become so unhealthy as to be discharged, and only four have been killed in battle.

Team Challenge! Working with a partner or a small group, explain how a Civil War correspondent on the front lines and a historian many years later might have used information from these and other primary sources to determine what the life of a soldier was like. What sort of sources would each use? What information might they have learned from these sources? Share your report with the class.

Take Notes

Literacy Skills: Sequence Use what you have read to complete the flowchart. Identify significant events during the last two years of the war (1863–1865). In the last box, describe the effect of the war on the nation. The first entry is completed for you.

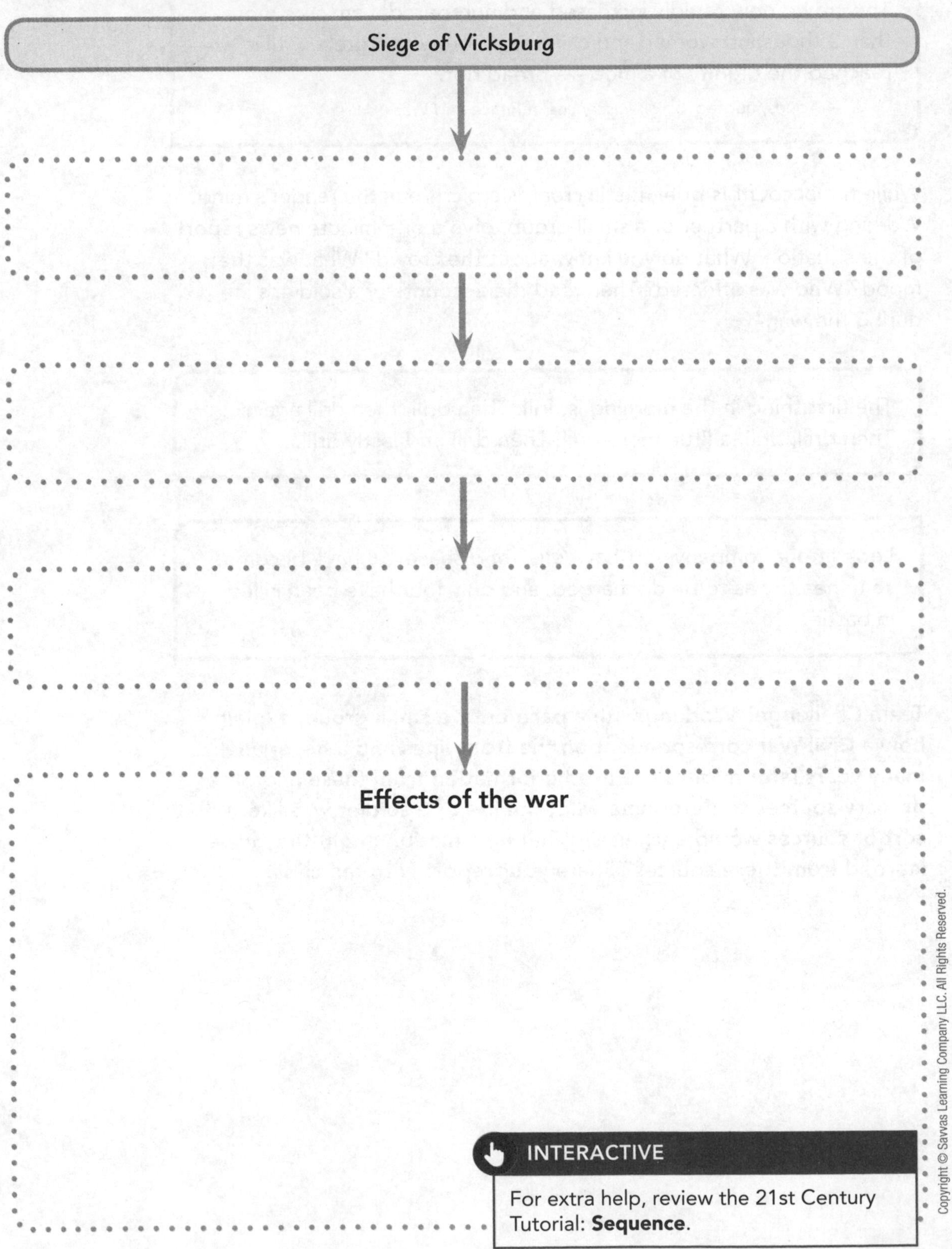

INTERACTIVE

For extra help, review the 21st Century Tutorial: **Sequence**.

Practice Vocabulary

Words in Context For each question below, write an answer that shows your understanding of the boldfaced key term.

1. Why was the meeting at **Appomattox Court House** significant?

2. How did **Pickett's Charge** change the course of the war?

3. Explain what happens during a military **siege**.

4. What happened at the **Battle of Gettysburg**?

5. What was Lincoln's goal in the **Gettysburg Address**?

Writing Workshop Informative Essay

As you read, build a response to this question: **What were the differences between the North and the South before, during, and after the Civil War? The prompts below will help you walk through the process.**

Lessons 1 and 2 Writing Tasks: Consider Your Purpose and Pick an Organizing Strategy (See Student Text, pages 397 and 409)

Describe what information you will provide to complete the task. Then, consider how you will present your information. Will you include visuals? Set out your plan below.

Lesson 3 Writing Task: Develop Your Thesis (See Student Text, page 421)

Write one sentence that describes your ideas on the differences between the North and the South before, during, and after the Civil War. This will be your thesis statement.

Lesson 4 Writing Task: Support Thesis with Details (See Student Text, page 429)

Review your thesis statement. Make any revisions you feel are necessary. List details from Lessons 1, 2, 3, and 4 describing the differences between the North and South. Use the table below to list these details.

North	South

Lesson 5 Writing Task: Write an Introduction (See Student Text, page 440)

Write the opening paragraph of your essay on another piece of paper. This opening paragraph should introduce your thesis and be clear and concise.

Lesson 6 Writing Task: Draft Your Essay (See Student Text, page 453)

Use the details you have been gathering to write a first draft of your essay about the differences between the North and South before, during, and after the Civil War.

Writing Task (See Student Text, page 455)

Using the draft you created, answer the following question in a five-paragraph informative essay: What were the differences between the North and the South before, during, and after the Civil War?

TOPIC 7

The Reconstruction Era Preview

Essential Question How should we handle conflict?

Before you begin this topic, think about the Essential Question by answering the following questions.

1. Check the ideas that you think are helpful ways of resolving conflict.

__compromising __shouting __speaking kindly

__listening to everyone __being open-minded __name-calling

__hitting __seeing another perspective

2. Preview the topic by skimming lesson titles, headings, and graphics. List ideas that you think might have been sources of conflict after the Civil War.

Timeline Skills

As you read, write and/or draw at least three events from the topic. Draw a line from each event to its correct position on the timeline.

1865	1870

Map Skills

Using maps throughout the topic, label the states listed below. Then, color and number each military district.

Alabama	Arkansas	Florida	Georgia
Louisiana	Mississippi	North Carolina	South Carolina
Texas	Virginia		

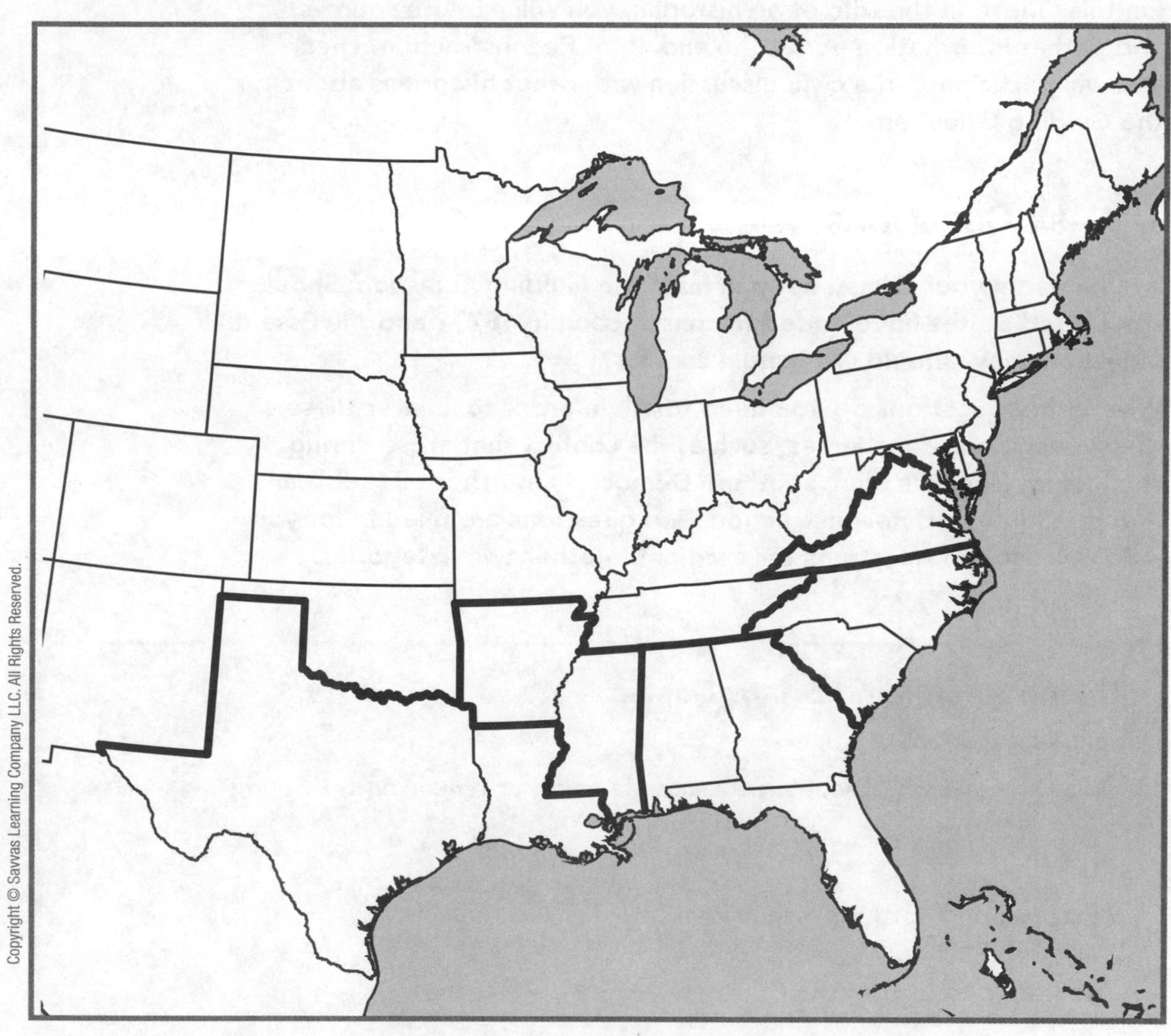

	1875	1880

The End of Reconstruction

On this Quest, in the role of an historian, you will explore sources and gather information about the ending of Reconstruction. Then, you will participate in a civic discussion with other historians about the Guiding Question.

 Ask Questions (See Student Text, page 460)

As you begin your Quest, keep in mind the Guiding Question: **Should the United States have ended Reconstruction in 1877?** and the Essential Question: **How should we handle conflict?**

What other questions do you need to ask in order to answer these questions? Consider themes, such as the conflict that arose during rebuilding, Lincoln's plan, southern Democrats, northern Republicans, and the South and Reconstruction. Two questions are filled in for you. Add at least two questions for each of the other two categories.

Theme Rebuilding Brings Conflict

Sample questions:

What plan did white southern Democrats favor for rebuilding the South?

What plan did northern Republicans favor?

Theme Lincoln's Plan

Theme Southern Democrats

Theme Northern Republicans

Theme The South and Reconstruction

Theme My Additional Questions

INTERACTIVE

For extra help with Step 1, review the 21st Century Tutorial: **Ask Questions**.

Quest CONNECTIONS

2 Investigate

As you read about the ending of Reconstruction, collect five connections to help you answer the Guiding Question. Three connections are already chosen for you.

Connect to Reconstruction Problems

Lesson 1 The Effects of the Civil War (See Student Text, page 462)

Here's a connection! Read this section in your text. What problems did the country face after the Civil War?

What problems would Reconstruction be expected to solve?

Connect to Frederick Douglass

Primary Source Frederick Douglass, "What the Black Man Wants"

(See Student Text, page 474)

Here's another connection! Frederick Douglass was an African American abolitionist, orator, and writer. What did Douglass want Reconstruction to achieve?

How did his goals for Reconstruction compare with those of others?

Connect to the End of Reconstruction

Lesson 4 New Restrictions on African American Rights

(See Student Text, page 487)

As troops withdrew from the South, what were some new ways that African Americans were prevented from exercising their rights?

Did Reconstruction successfully rebuild society?

It's Your Turn! Find two more connections. Fill in the title of your connections, then answer the questions. Connections may be images, primary sources, maps, or text.

Your Choice | Connect to

Location in text

What is the main idea of this connection?

What does this tell you about the events and legacy of Reconstruction?

Your Choice | Connect to

Location in text

What is the main idea of this connection?

What does this tell you about the events and legacy of Reconstruction?

3 Examine Primary Sources (See Student Text, page 490)

Examine the primary and secondary sources provided online or from your teacher. Fill in the chart to show how these sources provide further information about whether the United States should have ended Reconstruction in 1877. The first one is completed for you.

Should the United States have ended Reconstruction in 1877?	
Source	Yes or No? Why?
"Reconstruction Reassessed"	YES, *because freed slaves were unequipped to succeed with control of the corrupt southern government, making the South vulnerable to "Northern adventures."*
"The Supreme Court and the History of Reconstruction—and Vice-Versa"	
"The Use of Military Force to Protect the Gains of Reconstruction"	

INTERACTIVE

For extra help with Step 3, review the 21st Century Tutorial: **Compare Viewpoints**.

4 Discuss! (See Student Text, page 490)

Now that you have collected clues and explored documents about the end of Reconstruction, you are ready to discuss with your fellow historians the Guiding Question: Should the United States have ended Reconstruction in 1877? Follow the steps below, using the spaces provided to prepare for your discussion.

You will work with a partner in a small group of historians. Try to reach a consensus, a situation in which everyone is in agreement, on the question. Can you do it?

1. **Prepare Your Arguments** You will be assigned a position on the question, either YES or NO.

   My position:

   Work with your partner to review your Quest notes from the Quest Connections and Quest Sources.

   - If you were assigned YES, agree with your partner on what you think were the strongest arguments from Godkin and Foner.
   - If you were assigned NO, agree on what you think were the strongest arguments from Blair.

2. **Present Your Position** Those assigned YES will present their arguments and evidence first. As you listen, ask clarifying questions to gain information and understanding.

What is a Clarifying Question?	
These types of questions do not judge the person talking. They are only for the listener to be clear on what he or she is hearing.	
Example: Can you tell me more about that?	**Example:** You said [x]. Am I getting that right?

INTERACTIVE

For extra help with Step 4, review the 21st Century Tutorial: **Participate in a Discussion or Debate**.

While the opposite side speaks, take notes on what you hear in the space below.

3. **Switch!** Now NO and YES will switch sides. If you argued YES before, now you will argue NO. Work with your same partner and use your notes. Add any arguments and evidence from the clues and sources. Those *now* arguing YES go first.

When both sides have finished, answer the following:

Before **I started this discussion with my fellow historians, my opinion was that the United States**	***After*** **this discussion with my fellow historians, my opinion is that the United States**
____should have ended Reconstruction in 1877. ____should not have ended Reconstruction in 1877.	____should have ended Reconstruction in 1877. ____should not have ended Reconstruction in 1877.

4. **Point of View** Do you all agree on the answer to the Guiding Question?

- ____Yes
- ____No

If not, on what points do you all agree?

Take Notes

Literacy Skills: Identify Cause and Effect Use what you have read to complete the chart. Draw a line connecting the cause to the effect. The first one has been completed for you.

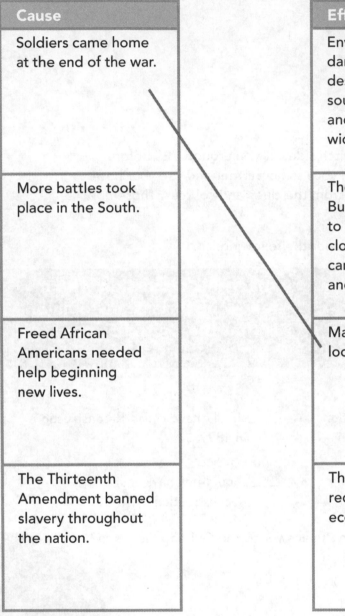

Cause	Effect
Soldiers came home at the end of the war.	Environmental damage, including destruction of southern farms and forests, was widespread.
More battles took place in the South.	The Freedmen's Bureau was created to help with food, clothing, medical care, education, and jobs.
Freed African Americans needed help beginning new lives.	Many people were looking for jobs.
The Thirteenth Amendment banned slavery throughout the nation.	The South had to redefine its social and economic systems.

INTERACTIVE

For extra help, review the 21st Century Tutorial: **Analyze Cause and Effect**.

Practice Vocabulary

Vocabulary Quiz Show **Some quiz shows ask a question and expect the contestant to give the answer. In other shows, the contestant is given an answer and must supply the question. If the blank is in the Question column, write the question that would result in the answer in the Answer column. If the question is supplied, write the answer.**

Question	Answer
1. What agency was established to help former slaves begin their new lives?	1.
2. What is a government pardon called?	2.
3.	3. freedmen
4.	4. Thirteenth Amendment
5. What name was given to describe the rebuilding of the nation?	5.

Quick Activity Debate with a Partner

In the roles of Congressional Republicans in 1864, debate with your partner the Ten Percent Plan versus the Wade-Davis Bill. Summarize your main ideas in this table.

Ten Percent Plan	Wade-Davis Bill

Did you know?

Remember! Under Lincoln's Ten Percent Plan, a southern state could form a new government after 10 percent of its voters swore an oath of loyalty to the United States. The new government would have to abolish slavery before the state could take part in national government again.

Did you know?

Remember! Under the Wade-Davis Bill, a majority of white men in each southern state had to swear loyalty to the Union, and anyone who had volunteered for the Confederacy was not allowed to vote or hold office.

Team Challenge! Reconstruction of the South was a long process. When Andrew Johnson became president, his plan for Reconstruction called for a majority of voters in each Southern state to pledge loyalty to the United States and to ratify the Thirteenth Amendment, which banned slavery throughout the nation. Discuss how Johnson's plan compared to the Ten Percent Plan and the Wade-Davis Bill. Given how Reconstruction played out, how might the adoption of one of these alternative plans have changed the course of events?

Take Notes

Literacy Skills: Identify Supporting Details Use what you have read to complete the table. Respond to each main idea with two supporting details. The first one has been completed for you.

Main Idea	Supporting Details
Even after the Thirteenth Amendment passed, the rights of African Americans were still extremely restricted.	• Under the black codes, freedmen were not allowed to vote, own guns, or serve on juries. • In some states, freedmen were only permitted to work as servants or farm laborers.
Radical Republicans wanted to improve civil rights and equality.	
The Fourteenth Amendment was an important step toward civil rights.	
Congress and President Johnson disagreed on how to proceed with Reconstruction.	
After the passage of the Fifteenth Amendment, there was still a long way to go to achieve civil rights.	

INTERACTIVE

For extra help, review the 21st Century Tutorial: **Support Ideas with Evidence**.

Practice Vocabulary

True or False? Decide whether each statement below is true or false. Circle T or F, and then explain your answer. Be sure to include the underlined vocabulary word in your explanation. The first one is done for you.

1. **T / F** The black codes were laws to help freedmen build new lives.
   False; The black codes were laws that severely restricted the rights of freed African Americans.

2. **T / F** Radical Republicans wanted to ensure freedmen received the right to vote.

3. **T / F** The Reconstruction Act of 1867 accepted all of the states back into the Union.

4. **T / F** The Fourteenth Amendment defined citizens as "all persons born or naturalized in the United States."

5. **T / F** The House of Representatives voted to impeach President Johnson because they agreed with him.

6. **T / F** The Fifteenth Amendment gave African American men over the age of 21 the right to vote.

Take Notes

Literacy Skills: Summarize Use what you have read to complete the table. In each box, list at least two details or ideas that describe the issue. Use your responses to summarize the lesson in three to five sentences. One has been completed for you.

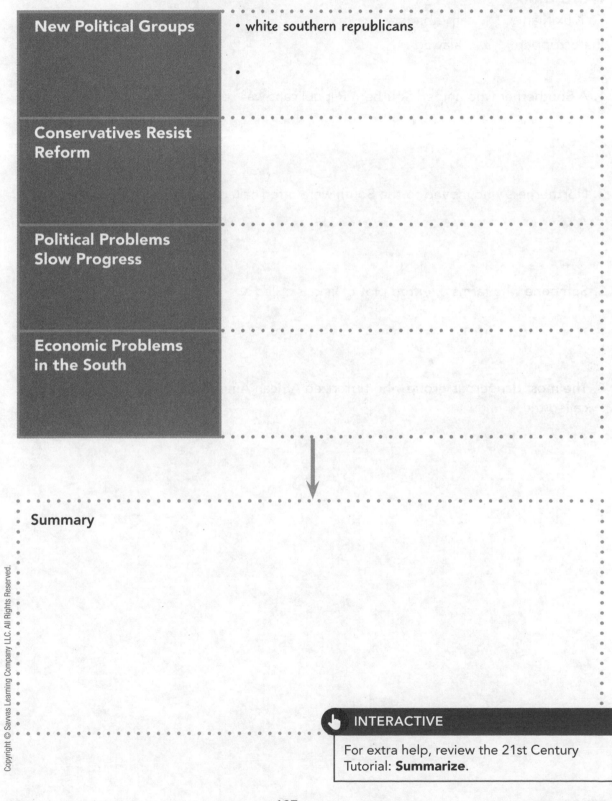

New Political Groups	• white southern republicans •
Conservatives Resist Reform	
Political Problems Slow Progress	
Economic Problems in the South	

Summary

INTERACTIVE

For extra help, review the 21st Century Tutorial: **Summarize**.

Practice Vocabulary

Sentence Builder **Finish the sentences below with a key term from this section. You may have to change the form of the words to complete the sentences.**

Word Bank

Ku Klux Klan	carpetbagger
sharecropper	scalawag

1. A Southerner who helped Southern Republicans was referred to as a

2. Northerners who moved to the South were often called

3. Someone who farms a rented plot of land is called a

4. The most dangerous group who terrorized African Americans is called the

Take Notes

Literacy Skills: Draw Conclusions Use what you have read to complete the diagram. List ways that African Americans in the South were prevented from exercising their rights during this time. Then, make conclusions about the impact these restrictions had on these citizens. The first detail has been completed for you.

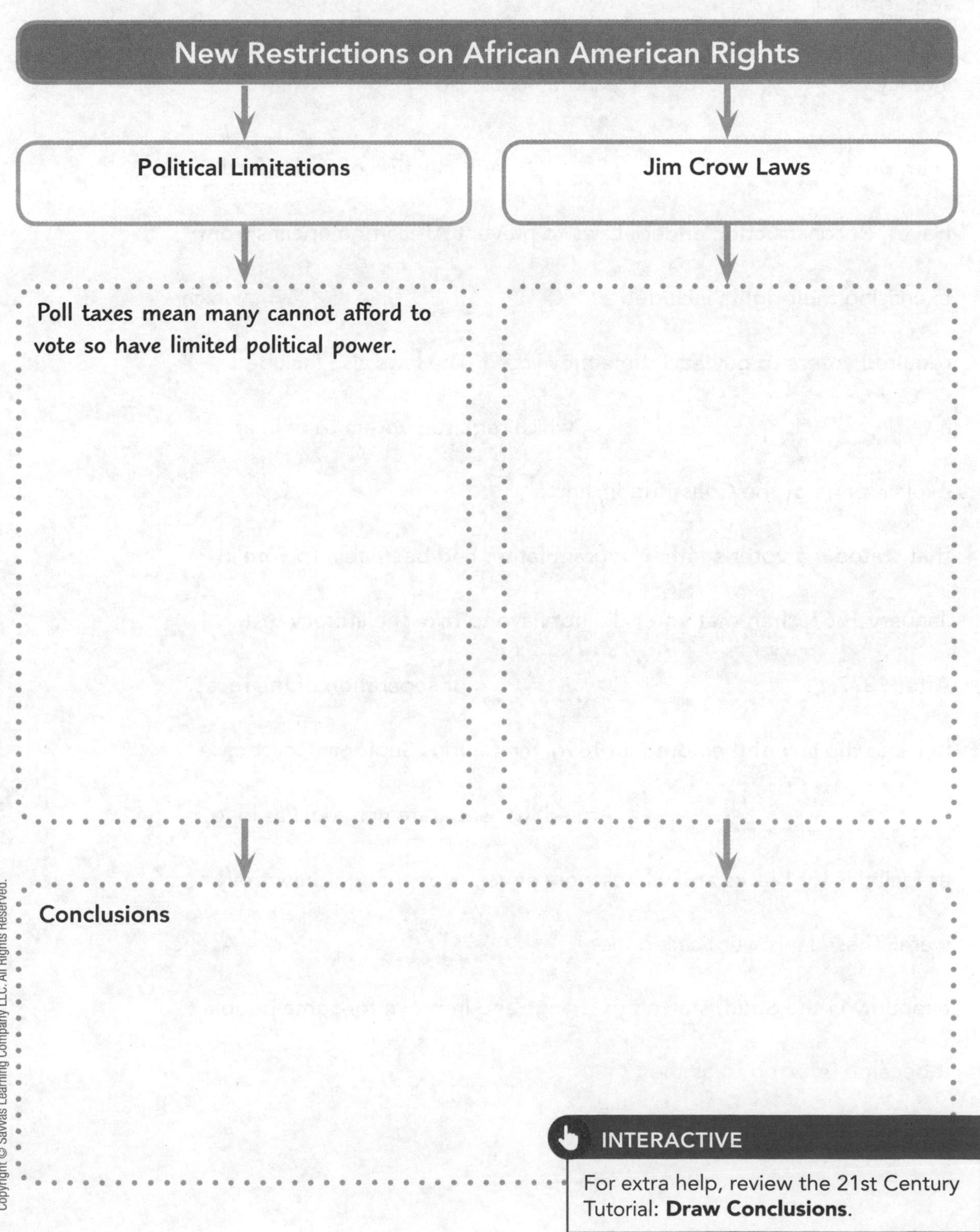

New Restrictions on African American Rights
Political Limitations
Jim Crow Laws
Poll taxes mean many cannot afford to vote so have limited political power.
Conclusions

INTERACTIVE

For extra help, review the 21st Century Tutorial: **Draw Conclusions**.

Practice Vocabulary

Use a Word Bank Choose one word from the word bank to fill in each blank. When you have finished, you will have a short summary of important ideas from the section.

Word Bank

segregation	"New South"	poll tax
Compromise of 1877	Jim Crow laws	*Plessy* v. *Ferguson*
literacy test	grandfather clause	

With the ______ and election of Rutherford B. Hayes, Reconstruction ended. Laws to prevent African Americans from exercising their rights included a ______, which required voters to pay each time they voted. The laws also included a ______, which required voters to read and explain parts of the Constitution, and a ______ that stated if a voter's father or grandfather had been able to vote in January 1867, then that voter did not have to take the literacy test. After 1877, ______, or separation of the races, became the law of the South. In 1896, the famous Supreme Court case ______ ruled that separate was legal as long as facilities for blacks and whites were equal, even though they rarely were. These laws were called the ______. As the economy in the South started to change and improve for some people, it became referred to as the ______.

Quick Activity Newspaper Editorial

Write a newspaper editorial supporting or opposing Samuel Tilden and the Democratic Party for choosing not to fight the commission's decision to award all of the disputed electors to Hayes. Use the chart below to help you organize your thinking.

> **Did you know?**
> An editorial is an opinion piece that uses facts to support an argument.

Introduction State your thesis.	
Evidence Support your claim with textual and factual evidence.	
Conclusion Help readers arrive at your conclusion based on the evidence you have provided.	

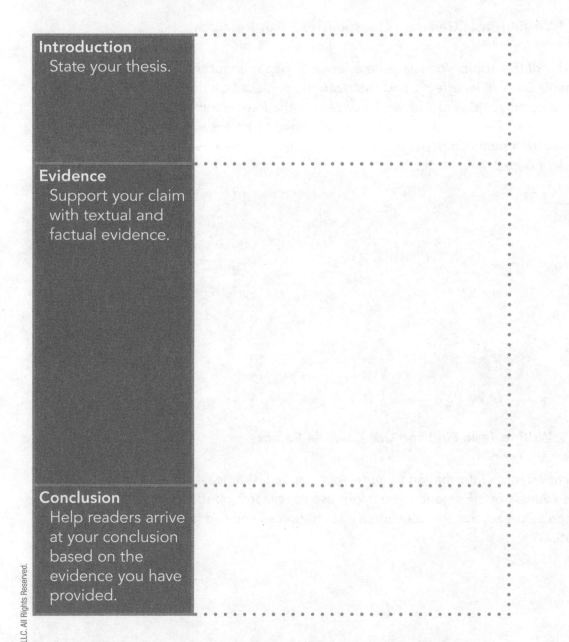

Team Challenge! Find a partner with a different opinion. Share your charts and talk about the differences. Practice listening to your partner's reasoning without arguing or making statements of your own. Instead, limit your responses to questions that help you better understand your partner's perspective and that help your partner develop and refine his or her opinion.

Writing Workshop Research Paper

As you read, build a response to the following research topic: The Freedmen's Bureau, its effects, and the restrictions placed on the rights and opportunities of African Americans in the Reconstruction-era South. The prompts below will help walk you through the process.

Lesson 1 Writing Task: Generate Questions to Focus Research

(See Student Text, page 467)

At the end of this topic, you will write a research paper about the Freedmen's Bureau, its effects, and the restrictions placed on the rights and opportunities of African Americans in the Reconstruction-era South. Make a list of questions that would need to be answered in order to write a research paper on this subject, such as: What was the Freedmen's Bureau?

Lesson 2 Writing Task: Find and Use Credible Sources

(See Student Text, page 473)

You will need more information to write your paper. List at least three credible sources of information you might use to research about the Freedmen's Bureau. Record the source information so you can find it again later.

Lesson 3 Writing Task: Support Ideas with Evidence

(See Student Text, page 482)

A thesis is a statement that a writer intends to support and prove. Write a thesis statement for your research paper. Then, outline your research paper by writing your main ideas. Under each main idea, write facts and other evidence that support that idea.

Thesis

Main Idea	Main Idea	Main Idea
Evidence	Evidence	Evidence

Lesson 4 Writing Task: Cite Sources (See Student Text, page 489)

Review the sources that you noted. Write citations for all of your sources, following the format provided by your teacher. Include the name of the article or text, the author, the publisher, the date of publication, and the web address (if applicable).

Writing Task (See Student Text, page 491)

Complete your research paper on the Freedmen's Bureau and its effects. Include a discussion of the limits placed on African Americans. Your paper should include a strong conclusion that summarizes your thesis and main ideas.

TOPIC 8

Industrial and Economic Growth Preview

Essential Question How did America's economy, industries, and population grow after the Civil War?

Before you begin this topic, think about the Essential Question by answering the following question.

1. List five words or ideas that come to mind when you think about the word *growth*. Based on your list, do you feel that growth is usually **positive** or **negative**? Circle the bold word that matches your opinion.

Timeline Skills

As you read, write and/or draw at least three events from the topic. Draw a line from each event to its correct position on the timeline.

1860	1870	1880

Map Skills

Using maps throughout the topic, label the map with the places listed. Then use different colors to shade states admitted before 1867 and states admitted from 1867 to 1912. Be sure to create a key for your map.

Arizona (1912)	Colorado (1876)	Idaho (1890)
Montana (1889)	Nebraska (1867)	New Mexico (1912)
North Dakota (1889)	Oklahoma (1907)	South Dakota (1889)
Utah (1896)	Washington (1889)	Wyoming (1890)
Canada	Mexico	Pacific Ocean
Gulf of Mexico		

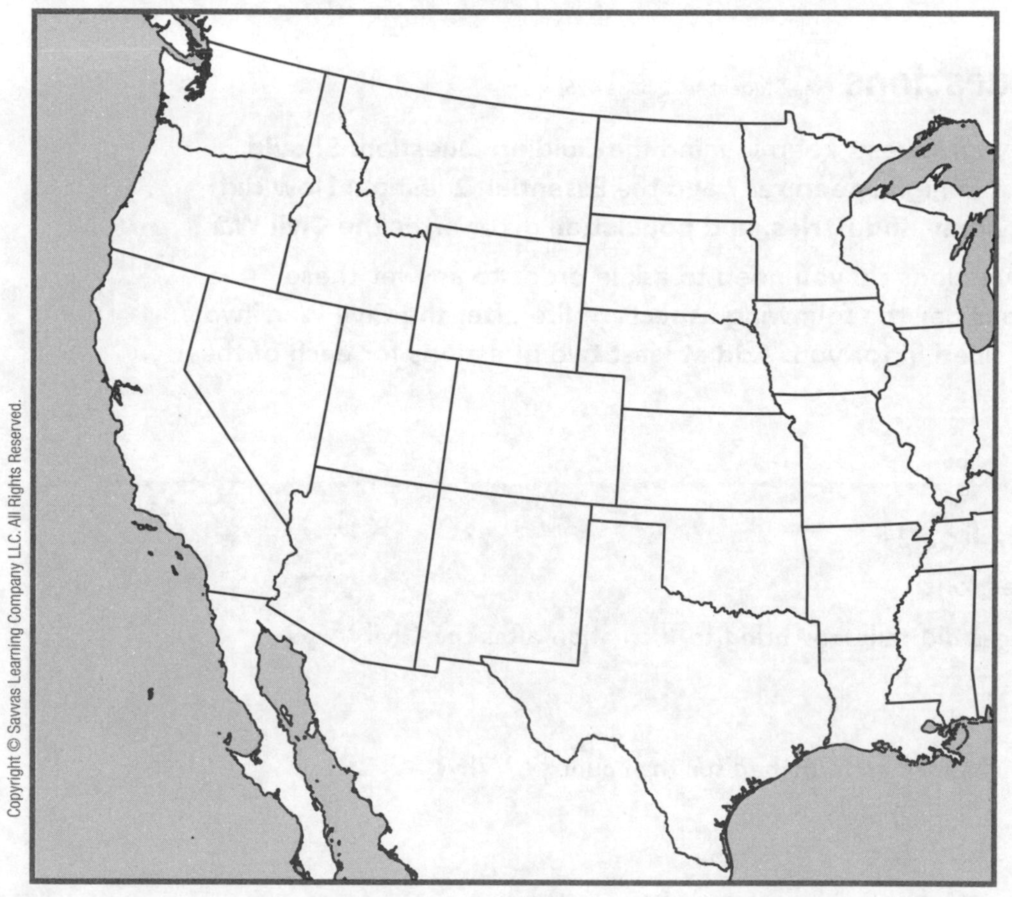

1890 1900 1910 1920

High-Speed Rail

On this Quest, you will explore sources and gather information about the benefits and drawbacks of high-speed rail. Then, in the role of a member of the U.S. House of Representative's Subcommittee on Railroads, you will participate in a civic discussion with other representatives about the Guiding Question.

1 Ask Questions (See Student Text, page 496)

As you begin your Quest, keep in mind the Guiding Question: **Should America invest in high-speed rail?** and the Essential Question: **How did America's economy, industries, and population grow after the Civil War?**

What other questions do you need to ask in order to answer these questions? Consider the following aspects of life after the Civil War. Two questions are filled in for you. Add at least two questions for each of the other categories.

Theme Railroads

Sample questions:

What changes did railroads bring to the nation after the Civil War?

Were these changes good or bad for the country? Why?

Theme Industry

Theme Population

Theme Western Agriculture

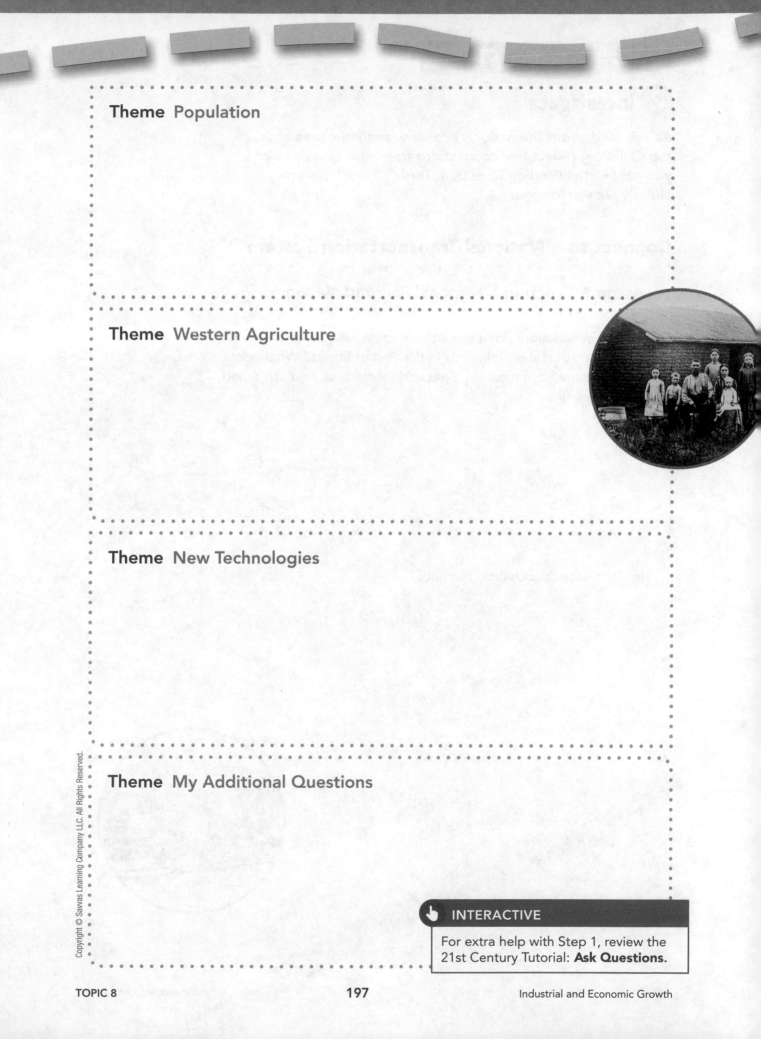

Theme New Technologies

Theme My Additional Questions

INTERACTIVE

For extra help with Step 1, review the 21st Century Tutorial: **Ask Questions.**

Quest CONNECTIONS

2 Investigate

As you read about the nation's economy and industries after the Civil War, collect five connections from your text to help you answer the Guiding Question. Three connections are already chosen for you.

Connect to a National Transportation System

Lesson 1 Creating a National Railroad Network

(See Student Text, page 503)

Here's a connection! What does this section tell you about the benefits of new transportation methods in the United States? What added benefits came from creating a network of rail lines that stretched across state lines?

How did networks change railroads?

Connect to Texas Ranchers and the Railroads

Lesson 2 How Did a Cattle Kingdom Start on the Plains?

(See Student Text, page 509)

Read about the Texas Cattle Kingdom and new opportunities for ranchers. In what way did the new railroads help bring about the cattle kingdom in Texas?

How does rail access change people's lives?

Connect to Thomas Edison

Primary Source Quotations from Thomas Edison

(See Student Text, page 555)

Here's another connection! Thomas Edison was a great inventor. How could new technology and inventions improve railroads?

What do you think Thomas Edison would have thought about the United States investing in high-speed rail? Explain your reasoning.

It's Your Turn! Find two more connections. Fill in the title of your connections, then answer the questions. Connections may be images, primary sources, maps, or text.

Your Choice | Connect to

Location in text

What is the main idea of this connection?

What does it tell you about whether the United States should invest in high-speed rail?

Your Choice | Connect to

Location in text

What is the main idea of this connection?

What does it tell you about whether the United States should invest in high-speed rail?

3 Examine Primary Sources (See Student Text, page 556)

Examine the primary and secondary sources provided online or from your teacher. Fill in the chart to show how these sources provide further information about whether America should invest in high-speed rail. The first one is completed for you.

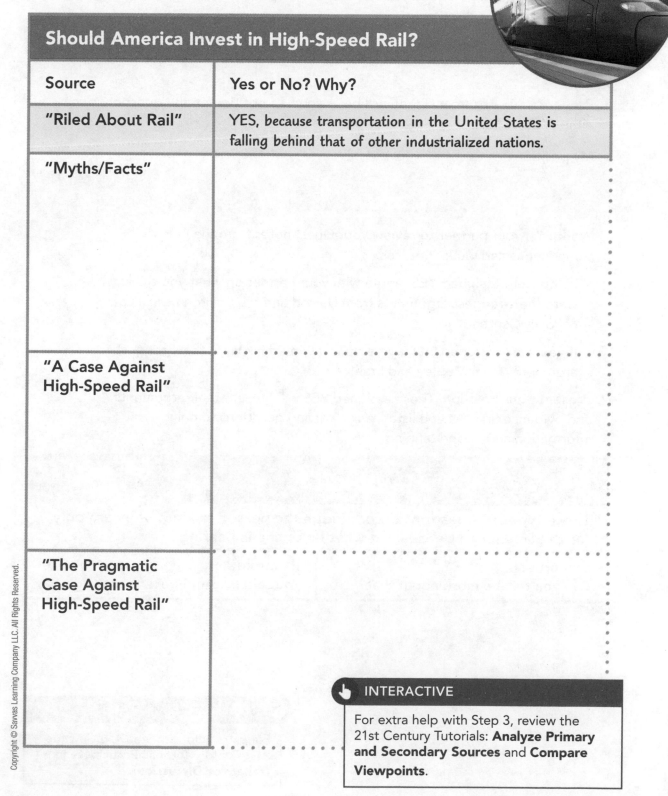

Should America Invest in High-Speed Rail?	
Source	**Yes or No? Why?**
"Riled About Rail"	YES, *because transportation in the United States is falling behind that of other industrialized nations.*
"Myths/Facts"	
"A Case Against High-Speed Rail"	
"The Pragmatic Case Against High-Speed Rail"	

INTERACTIVE

For extra help with Step 3, review the 21st Century Tutorials: **Analyze Primary and Secondary Sources** and **Compare Viewpoints**.

Quest FINDINGS

4 Discuss! (See Student Text, page 556)

Now that you have collected clues and explored sources about high-speed rail, you are ready to discuss with your fellow representatives the Guiding Question: Should America invest in high-speed rail? Follow the steps below, using the spaces provided to prepare for your discussion.

You will work with a partner in a small group of representatives. Try to reach consensus, a situation in which everyone is in agreement, on the question. Can you do it?

1. **Prepare Your Arguments** You will be assigned a position on the question, either YES or NO.

   My position:

   Work with your partner to review your Quest notes from the Quest Connections and Quest Sources.

   - If you were assigned YES, agree with your partner on what you think were the strongest arguments from Harrod and the Environmental Law & Policy Center.
   - If you were assigned NO, agree on what you think were the strongest arguments from Mobley and Staley.

2. **Present Your Position** Those assigned YES will present their arguments and evidence first. As you listen, ask clarifying questions to gain information and understanding.

What is a Clarifying Question?	
These types of questions do not judge the person talking. They are only for the listener to be clear on what he or she is hearing.	
Example: **Can you tell me more about that?**	**Example:** **You said [x]. Am I getting that right?**

INTERACTIVE

For extra help with Step 4, review the 21st Century Tutorial: **Participate in a Debate or Discussion**.

While the opposite side speaks, take notes on what you hear in the space below.

3. **Switch!** Now NO and YES will switch sides. If you argued YES before, now you will argue NO. Work with your same partner and use your notes. Add any arguments and evidence from the clues and sources. Those *now* arguing YES go first.

When both sides have finished, answer the following:

Before I started this discussion with my fellow representatives, my opinion was that America	*After* this discussion with my fellow representatives, my opinion is that America
____should invest in high-speed rail.	____should invest in high-speed rail.
____should not invest in high-speed rail.	____should not invest in high-speed rail.

4. **Point of View** Do you all agree on the answer to the Guiding Question?

- ____Yes
- ____No

If not, on what points do you all agree?

Take Notes

Literacy Skills: Identify Cause and Effect Use what you have read to complete the flowcharts. In each space, write an effect of the event provided and support your answer with details from the text. The first one has been started for you.

Mining Booms in the West

↓

Environmental Problems

- Forests are cut down.
- Mines and towns pollute water sources.

Completion of the Transcontinental Railroad

↓

INTERACTIVE

For extra help, review the 21st Century Tutorial: **Analyze Cause and Effect**.

Practice Vocabulary

Vocabulary Quiz Show **Some quiz shows ask a question and expect the contestant to give the answer. In other shows, the contestant is given an answer and must supply the question. If the blank is in the Question column, write the question that would result in the answer in the Answer column. If the question is supplied, write the answer.**

Question	**Answer**
1. What word is used to describe the width of railroad track?	1.
2. What was a discount offered by railroads to big customers?	2.
3.	3. lode
4.	4. vigilante
5. What did the railroad owners form to end competition, which enabled them to fix high prices?	5.
6. What is a system of connected railroad lines?	6.
7.	7. transcontinental railroad
8.	8. subsidy
9.	9. consolidate

Take Notes

Literacy Skills: Classify and Categorize Use what you have read to complete the chart. In each space write details from the text that describe the type of challenge. The first one has been completed for you.

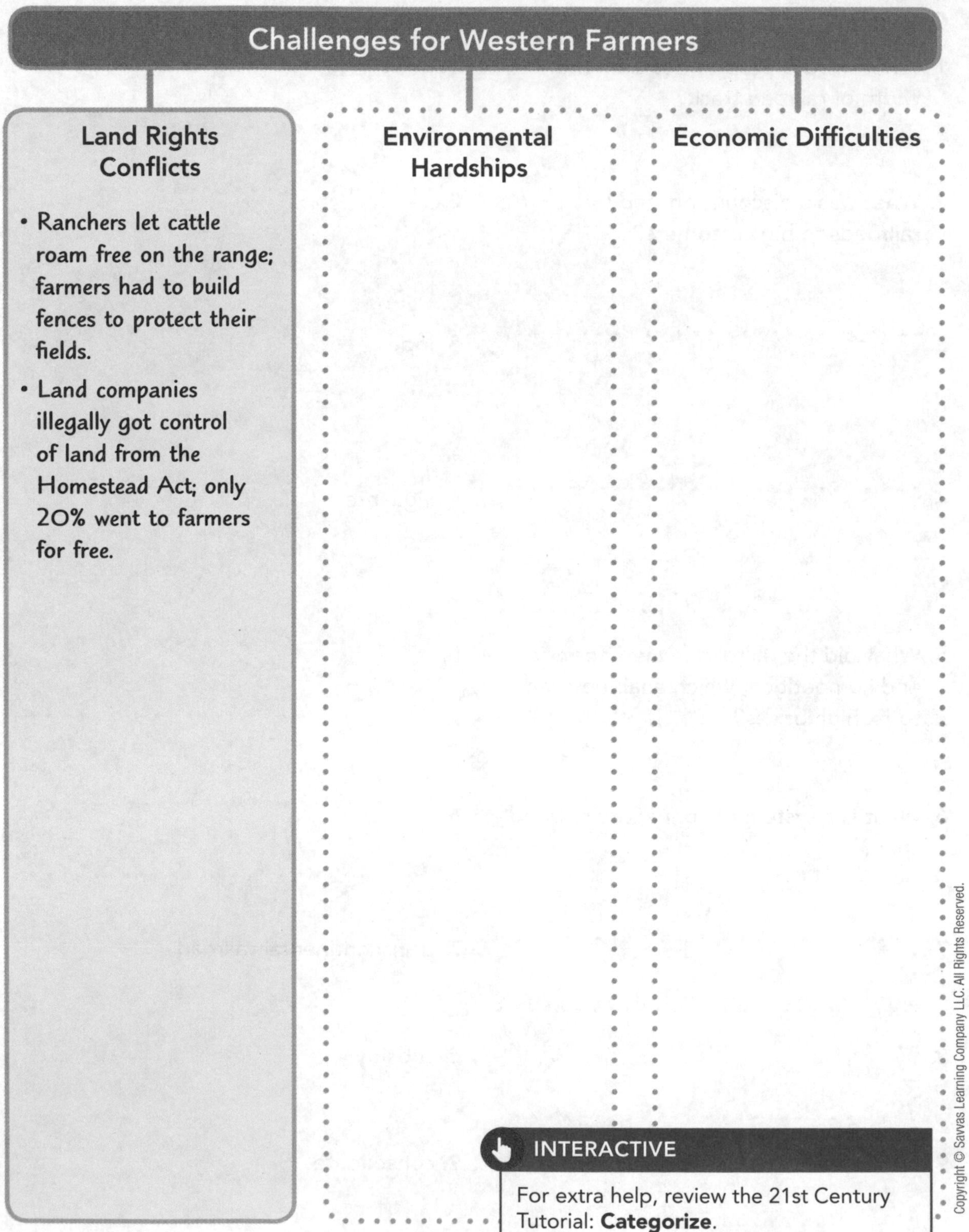

Challenges for Western Farmers
Land Rights Conflicts
• Ranchers let cattle roam free on the range; farmers had to build fences to protect their fields.
• Land companies illegally got control of land from the Homestead Act; only 20% went to farmers for free.
Environmental Hardships
Economic Difficulties

INTERACTIVE

For extra help, review the 21st Century Tutorial: **Categorize**.

Practice Vocabulary

Word Map **Study the word map for the word *cow town*. Characteristics are words or phrases that relate to the term in the center of the word map. Non-characteristics are words and phrases not associated with that term. Use the blank word map to explore the meaning of the word *sodbuster*. Then make word maps of your own for these words: *vaquero, cattle drive, cooperative, Morrill Acts, wholesale,* and *inflation*.**

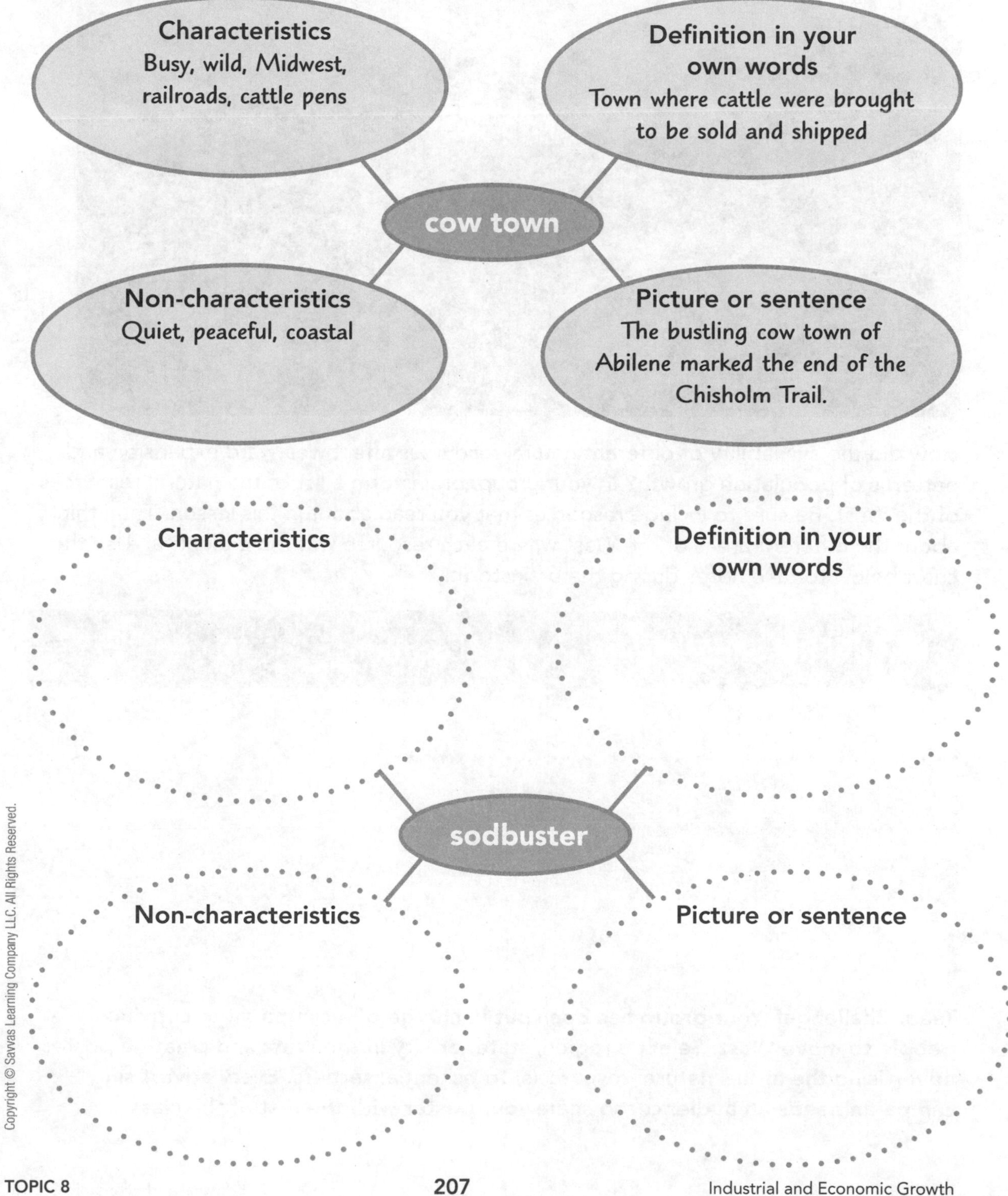

Quick Activity Westward Bound!

With a partner or small group, examine this illustration depicting the Oklahoma Land Rush. As you look at the picture, discuss possible reasons why people were so eager to move to Oklahoma. What natural resources might have made Oklahoma a good place to settle?

How did the availability of different natural resources affect westward expansion and patterns of population growth? In your group, brainstorm a list of the natural resources of the West. Be sure to include resources that you read about in this lesson. Then think about the different areas of the West where each resource was most plentiful. Use the chart below to take notes during the brainstorm.

Natural Resource	Locations

Team Challenge! Your group has been put in charge of a campaign to convince people to move West. Select a region, state, or city in the West and create a poster advertising the area's natural resource(s) to potential settlers. Every advertising campaign needs an audience, so share your poster with the rest of the class.

Take Notes

Literacy Skills: Summarize Use what you have read to complete the table. Include at least one detail from the text for each subtopic listed. The first one has been completed for you. Then, use the information you have gathered to create a summary statement that answers the question provided.

Plains Life Before White Settlement	Changes to Plains Indian Life	Plains Conflicts with White Settlers
Lifestyle: Survival depended on agriculture, hunting, and after 1680, horses. Homes were semi-permanent, and tepees were used when following bison herds.	**Decline of Bison:**	**Sand Creek Massacre:**
Social Structure: Women made the homes, gathered, taught, and were caregivers. Some governed and hunted. Men hunted, taught boys, and were warriors. Some governed and were military and spiritual leaders.	**Reservations:**	**Battle of Little Big Horn:**

Summary:

INTERACTIVE

For extra help, review the 21st Century Tutorial: **Summarize**.

Practice Vocabulary

Sentence Builder Finish the sentences below with a key term from this section. You may have to change the form of the words to complete the sentences.

Word Bank

travois	tepee	jerky
corral	reservation	allotment

1. Before horses were brought to the Great Plains, the best way to hunt bison was to herd them into a(n) ______.

2. The Dawes Act called for the ______ of reservation land to individual American Indian families.

3. When Plains Indians needed to move their villages to follow the bison, they loaded their belongings onto ______.

4. Bison meat that has been cut up and dried is called ______.

5. According to the terms of the Fort Laramie Treaty of 1868, the Lakotas and Arapahos would live on ______.

6. When Plains Indians were following bison herds, they lived in tents called ______.

Take Notes

Literacy Skills: Cite Evidence **Use what you have read to complete the flowchart. Provide at least one detail for each subheading. Then, use the details you have gathered to draw a conclusion about the question provided. The first column has been completed for you.**

Andrew Carnegie

Background:

After seeing the Bessemer process at work, he was inspired to borrow money and start a steel mill.

Business Strategy:

He used profits to buy out rivals.

His vertical integration involved buying iron mines, railroads, steamships, and warehouses to control all parts of the steel industry.

Philosophy:

Trusts are good and too much competition is harmful.

The rich have a duty to help the poor ("gospel of wealth").

John D. Rockefeller

Background:

Business Strategy:

Philosophy:

Draw a Conclusion: Why were business people like Carnegie and Rockefeller so successful?

INTERACTIVE

For extra help, review the 21st Century Tutorial: **Support Ideas With Evidence**.

Practice Vocabulary

True or False? Decide whether each statement below is true or false. Circle T or F, and then explain your answer. Be sure to include the underlined vocabulary word in your explanation. The first one is done for you.

1. T / F Capitalism is an economic system in which businesses are owned by the government.
False; Capitalism is an economic system in which businesses are owned by private citizens.

2. T / F Dividends are shares of a corporation's profit that are paid to stockholders.

3. T / F A business that is owned by investors is called a corporation.

4. T / F The principle of scarcity is that the economy improves when businesses and customers have few choices.

5. T / F A trust is a group of corporations run by a single individual.

6. T / F The Standard Oil trust controlled such a significant part of the oil industry that it formed a monopoly.

7. T / F Stock is the income that a business earns after it recovers costs.

Take Notes

Literacy Skills: Analyze Text Structure Use what you have read to complete the outline about the labor movement. Be sure to include significant headings, subheadings, and supporting details in your outline. The first section has been completed for you.

I. Changes in Working Conditions

A. Child Labor

1. Children worked long hours at dangerous jobs.
2. Child laborers were often uneducated.

B. Dangerous Workplaces

1. Factories, sweatshops, mines, and steel mills paid workers low wages for long hours in dangerous conditions.
2. The government did not regulate businesses to protect workers.

II.

INTERACTIVE

For extra help, review the 21st Century Tutorial: **Identify Main Ideas and Details.**

Practice Vocabulary

Sentence Revision **Revise each sentence so that the underlined vocabulary word is used logically. Be sure not to change the vocabulary word. The first one is done for you.**

1. Anarchists are people who support organized government.
   Anarchists are people who are opposed to all forms of organized government.

2. Strikebreakers are hired to negotiate with striking workers.

3. In sweatshops, people work long hours in poor conditions to receive overtime pay.

4. A trade union unites workers from many different trades.

5. The Triangle Fire led to a decrease in the number of safety laws protecting factory workers.

6. In collective bargaining, individual workers negotiate through discussions with multiple levels of management.

Take Notes

Literacy Skills: Identify Supporting Details Study the concept web for *transatlantic communication*. Use what you have read to complete the concept web for *telephone*. Then make concept webs of your own for *refrigeration*, *automobile*, and *airplane*.

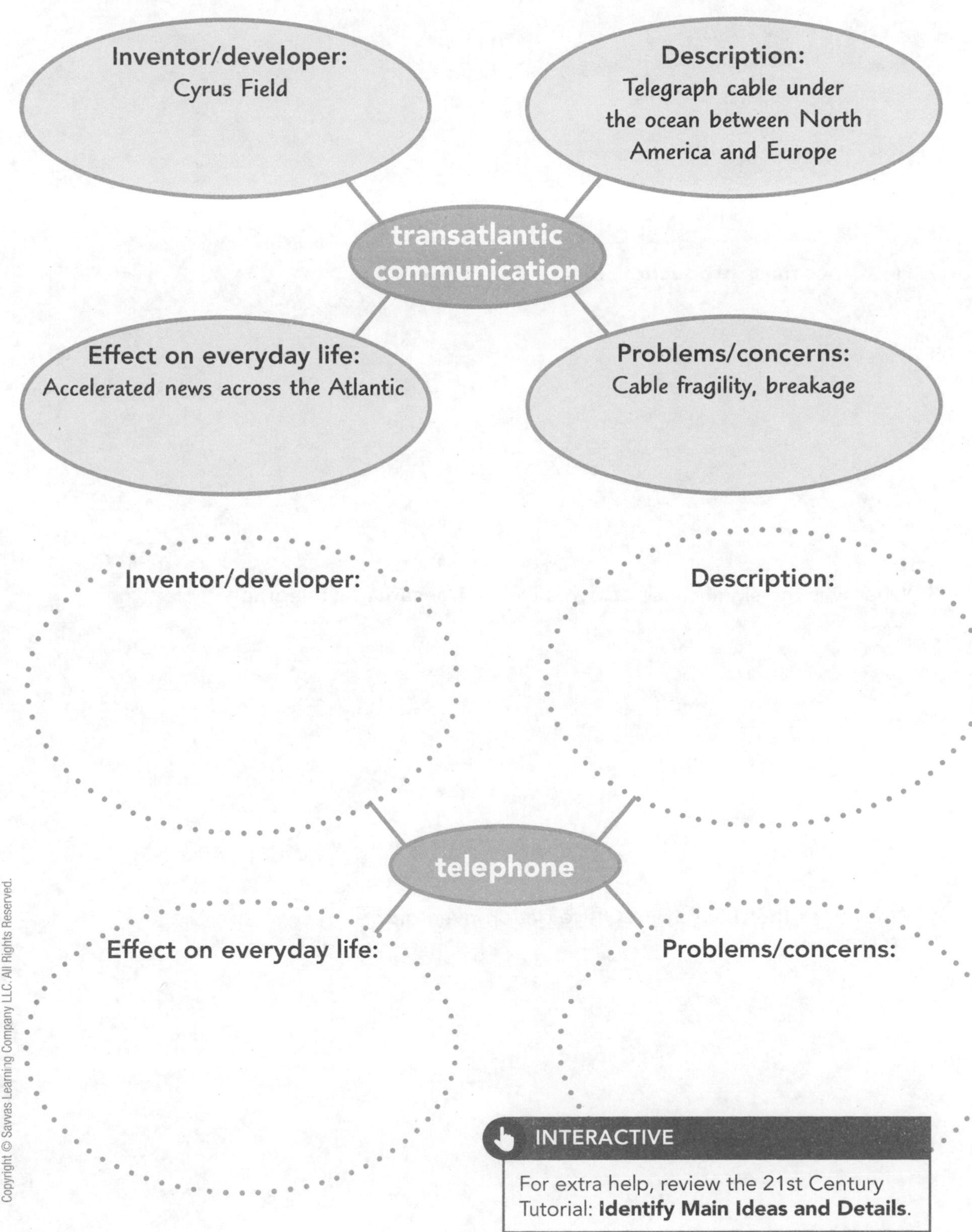

INTERACTIVE

For extra help, review the 21st Century Tutorial: **Identify Main Ideas and Details**.

Practice Vocabulary

Words in Context For each question below, write an answer that shows your understanding of the boldfaced key term.

1. How did Ford's use of the **moving assembly line** affect production industries?

2. How does **mass production** affect product prices?

3. What was the significance of Cyrus Field's **transatlantic** telegraph cable?

4. What does the U.S. **Patent** Office do for inventors?

Quick Activity Inventing for Change

With a partner or small group, examine these photos and brainstorm ways that the invention of the automobile forever changed the United States.

How did automobiles affect businesses and the economy? How did automobiles affect the landscape? What forms of transportation did the automobile replace? How did the automobile change everyday life?

Team Challenge! As a group, select one of the other inventions from the lesson and create an exhibit for a virtual Museum of Invention. Your group's museum exhibit should give information about the inventor, describe the invention, and inform viewers about the significance of the invention. Consider: How did the invention change people's lives in the 1800s? Does it still affect people's lives today? Display your results with the rest of the class, and take a "museum tour" around the classroom!

Writing Workshop Arguments

As you read, build a response to this question: What role should the government play in the development of a nation's infrastructure? The prompts below will help walk you through the process.

Lesson 1 Writing Task: Introduce Claims (See Student Text, page 507)

Write two sentences that summarize your position on the government's role in creating a national infrastructure. This will be the position you defend in the argument you will write at the end of the topic.

Lesson 2 and 4 Writing Task: Support Claims and Use Credible Sources
(See Student Text, pages 519 and 539)

As you read lessons 2 and 4, pay attention to details or concepts that support your claim. In the table below, write three sentences that support your claim and cite trustworthy sources for your information.

Supporting Details and Concepts	Source
1.	1.
2.	2.
3.	3.

Lesson 3 Writing Task: Distinguish Claims from Opposing Claims A well-constructed argument takes into account the views of the opposing side. In this table, first write a sentence summarizing the opposing claim. On the left, provide reasons and evidence that the opposing side might use to support their claim. On the right, express how your evidence differs.

Opposing Claim:	
Opposing Reasons and Evidence	How My Evidence Differs

Lesson 5 Writing Task: Shape Tone Look back at what you've written so far and analyze your tone. Does the argument make you feel angry or inspired? Does your writing seem emotional or calm? Determine the type of tone you would like your argument to have. Then revise the claim you wrote in lesson 1 so that it reflects the tone you want.

Lesson 6 Writing Task: Write a Conclusion The conclusion of your essay should do more than summarize what you have already said; it should restate your claim in powerful and persuasive ways that your reader will remember. Review all your reasons and evidence. Then, use a separate sheet of paper to write a draft conclusion for your argument using the tone you've identified.

Writing Task Using the outline you have created, write a five-paragraph argument that expresses your position on the question: What role should the government play in the development of a nation's infrastructure?

The Progressive Era Preview

Essential Question What can individuals do to affect society?

Before you begin this topic, think about the Essential Question by answering the following question.

List the ways you have made a positive impact on the people you know or your community. Circle the one of which you are most proud.

Timeline Skills

As you read, write and/or draw at least three events from the topic. Draw a line from each event to its correct position on the timeline.

1860	1870	1880

Map Skills

Using maps throughout the topic, color each state based on the percentage of its residents in 1900 who had been born in other countries. Create a key for your map.

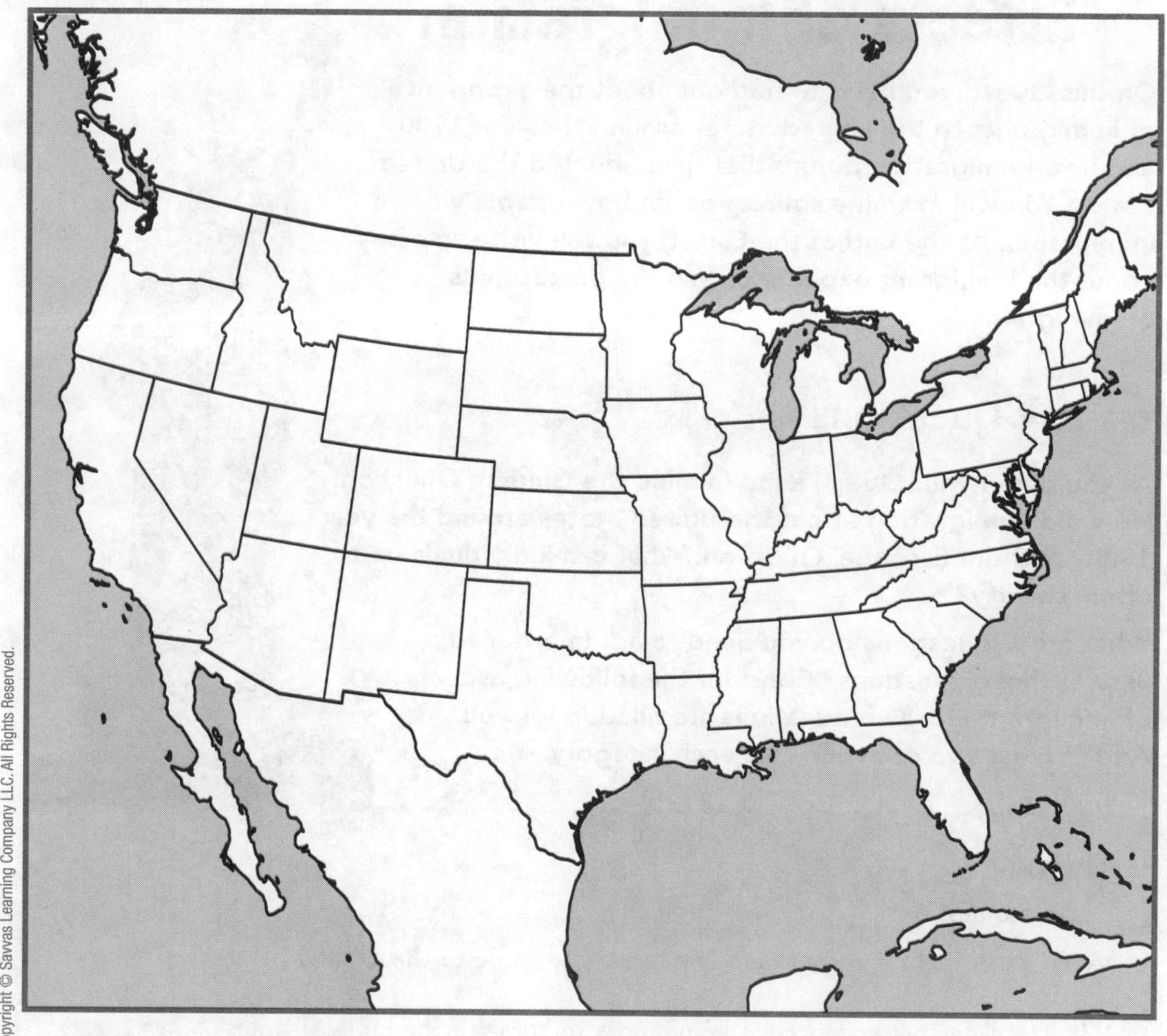

1890 | 1900 | 1910 | 1920

Quest

Document-Based Writing Inquiry

Effects of Immigration

On this Quest, you need to find out about the experience of immigrants to the United States around the year 1900 and how immigration during that time affected the United States. You will examine sources about how people viewed immigrants. At the end of the Quest, you will write an essay about the immigrant experience and the perceptions of immigrants.

1 Ask Questions (See Student Text, page 562)

As you begin your Quest, keep in mind the Guiding Question: **How did immigration affect the United States around the year 1900?** and the Essential Question: **What can individuals do to affect society?**

What other questions do you need to ask in order to answer these questions? Consider the following aspects of immigrant life. Two questions are filled in for you. Add at least two questions for each category.

Theme Opportunity

Sample questions:

What push factors encouraged immigrants to come to the United States?

What pull factors encouraged immigrants to come to the United States?

Theme Hardship

Theme Culture

Theme Nativism

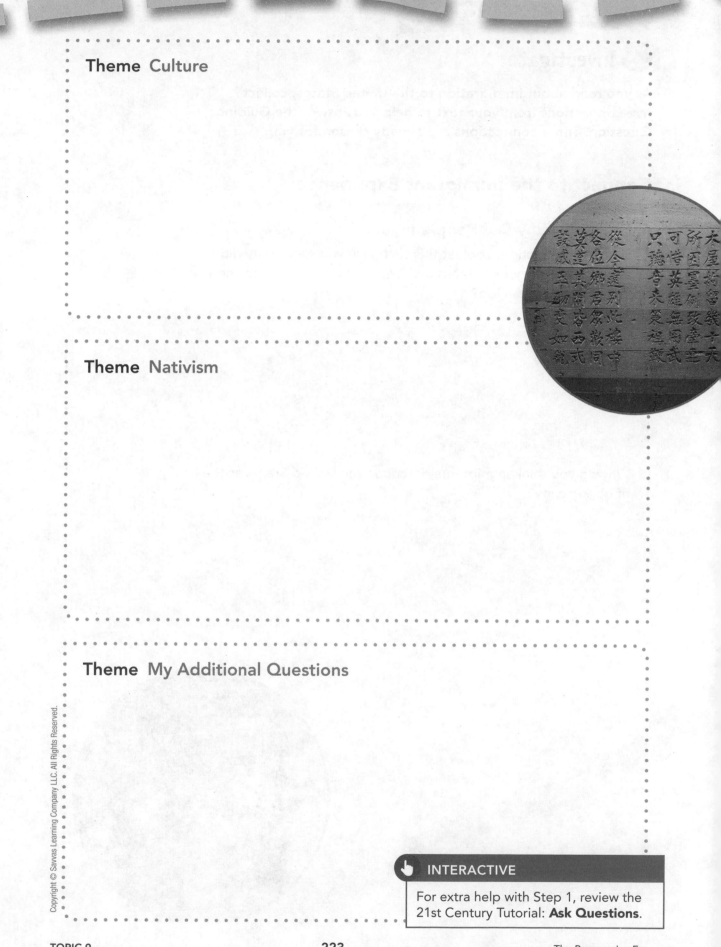

Theme My Additional Questions

INTERACTIVE

For extra help with Step 1, review the 21st Century Tutorial: **Ask Questions**.

Quest CONNECTIONS

2 Investigate

As you read about immigration to the United States, collect five connections from your text to help you answer the Guiding Question. Three connections are already chosen for you.

Connect to the Immigrant Experience

Lesson 1 Why Did People Immigrate? (See Student Text, page 564)

Here's a connection! Look at this section in your text. Why did new immigrants take jobs in factories? Why was it so important for a new immigrant to find a job?

Why do you think immigrants described the United States as the land of opportunity?

Connect to Urbanization

Lesson 2 What Was the Settlement House Movement?

(See Student Text, page 577)

Here's another connection! What does this section tell you about the connection between immigration and urbanization? Why did settlement houses offer services to the poor?

What services did volunteers for the Hull House offer people in the slum community?

Connect to Immigration Policies

Lesson 5 The Government Restricts Asian Immigration

(See Student Text, page 605)

What does this connection tell you about the experience of Asian immigrants in the United States? How were they treated?

How did the policy toward Japanese immigration change during this time?

It's Your Turn! Find two more connections. Fill in the title of your connections, then answer the questions. Connections may be images, primary sources, maps, or text.

Your Choice | Connect to

Location in text

What is the main idea of this connection?

What does it tell you about immigration in the United States around the year 1900?

Your Choice | Connect to

Location in text

What is the main idea of this connection?

What does it tell you about immigration in the United States around the year 1900?

3 Examine Primary Sources (See Student Text, page 620)

Examine the primary and secondary sources provided online or from your teacher. Fill in the chart to show how these sources provide further information about how immigration affected the United States around the year 1900. The first one is completed for you.

Source	Immigration affected the United States by . . .
Constitution of the Immigration Restriction League	leading some people to form groups that opposed immigration. They wanted to limit or curtail immigration.
The Promised Land	
The Biography of a Chinaman	
The Chinese Exclusion Conference	
Working in a Sweatshop	

INTERACTIVE

For extra help with Step 3, review the 21st Century Tutorial: **Analyze Primary and Secondary Sources**.

4 Write Your Essay (See Student Text, page 620)

Now it's time to put together all of the information you have gathered and use it to write your essay.

1. **Prepare to Write** You have collected connections and explored primary and secondary sources that show how immigration affected the United States around the year 1900. Look through your notes and decide which facts you would like to include in your essay. Record them here.

Facts about Immigration

2. **Write a Draft** Using evidence from the information in the textbook and the primary and secondary sources you explored, write a draft of your essay. Be sure to write about both the experience immigrants had and what some Americans believed about them. Include details from the evidence in the material you've studied in this Quest.

3. **Share with a Partner** Exchange your draft with a partner. Tell your partner what you like about his or her draft and suggest any improvements.

4. **Finalize Your Essay** Revise your essay. Correct any grammatical or spelling errors.

5. **Reflect on the Quest** Think about your experience completing this topic's Quest. What did you learn about the immigrant experience and reaction to immigration? What questions do you still have about immigration? How will you answer them?

Reflections

INTERACTIVE

For extra help with Step 4, review the 21st Century Tutorial: **Write an Essay**.

Take Notes

Literacy Skills: Summarize Use what you have read to complete the outline, summarizing the main ideas of the lesson. Some parts have been completed for you.

I. Why Did People Immigrate?
   A. Push factors
      scarcity of land, political and religious persecution, political unrest
   B. Pull factors
      industrial jobs in U.S., promise of freedom

II. What Was an Immigrant's Journey Like?
   A.
   B.

III. What was the Immigrant Experience in America?
   A.
   B.

IV. Why Did Nativists Oppose Immigration?
   A.
   B.

INTERACTIVE

For extra help, review the 21st Century Tutorial: **Summarize**.

Practice Vocabulary

True or False? Decide whether each statement below is true or false. Circle T or F, and then explain your answer. Be sure to include the underlined vocabulary word in your explanation. The first one is done for you.

1. **T / F** A pogrom was an organized attack on a Jewish village.
   True; The pogroms were supported by the Russian government.

2. **T / F** A push factor is a condition that attracts immigrants to a new area.

3. **T / F** The Chinese Exclusion Act barred Chinese laborers from entering the United States after its passage in 1882.

4. **T / F** The first generation of immigrants to arrive in America went through a process called acculturation.

5. **T / F** A pull factor is a condition that drives people from their homes.

6. **T / F** People who wanted to limit immigration and preserve the country for native-born, white Protestants were called nativists.

7. **T / F** Immigrants could have afforded nice quarters on ships that sailed to America, but they chose to stay in steerage to save money.

Quick Activity Write a Song

Throughout American history, musicians have written songs about immigrants. Use these pictures to get some ideas for writing your own immigration song, or find inspiration by searching the Internet for these songs and reading the lyrics.

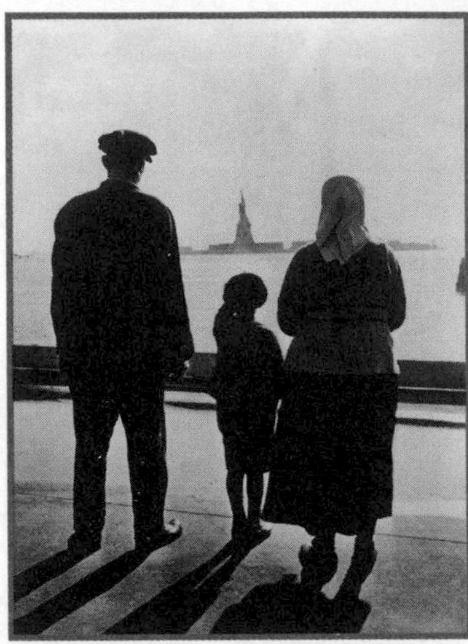

◀ Many families sailed to America at the turn of the 20th century looking for a better life.

▲ Immigrant children often worked in factories before laws were passed to forbid this practice.

Team Challenge! After everybody in your class posts their songs around the classroom, read the songs. Discuss with your classmates why they chose to write what they did. You also might want to talk about the melody they will use with their songs. Will it be happy or sad? Why?

Take Notes

Literacy Skills: Identify Cause and Effect **Use what you have read to complete the flowcharts. In each lower box, enter an effect that resulted from the cause in the top box. The first one has been partially completed for you.**

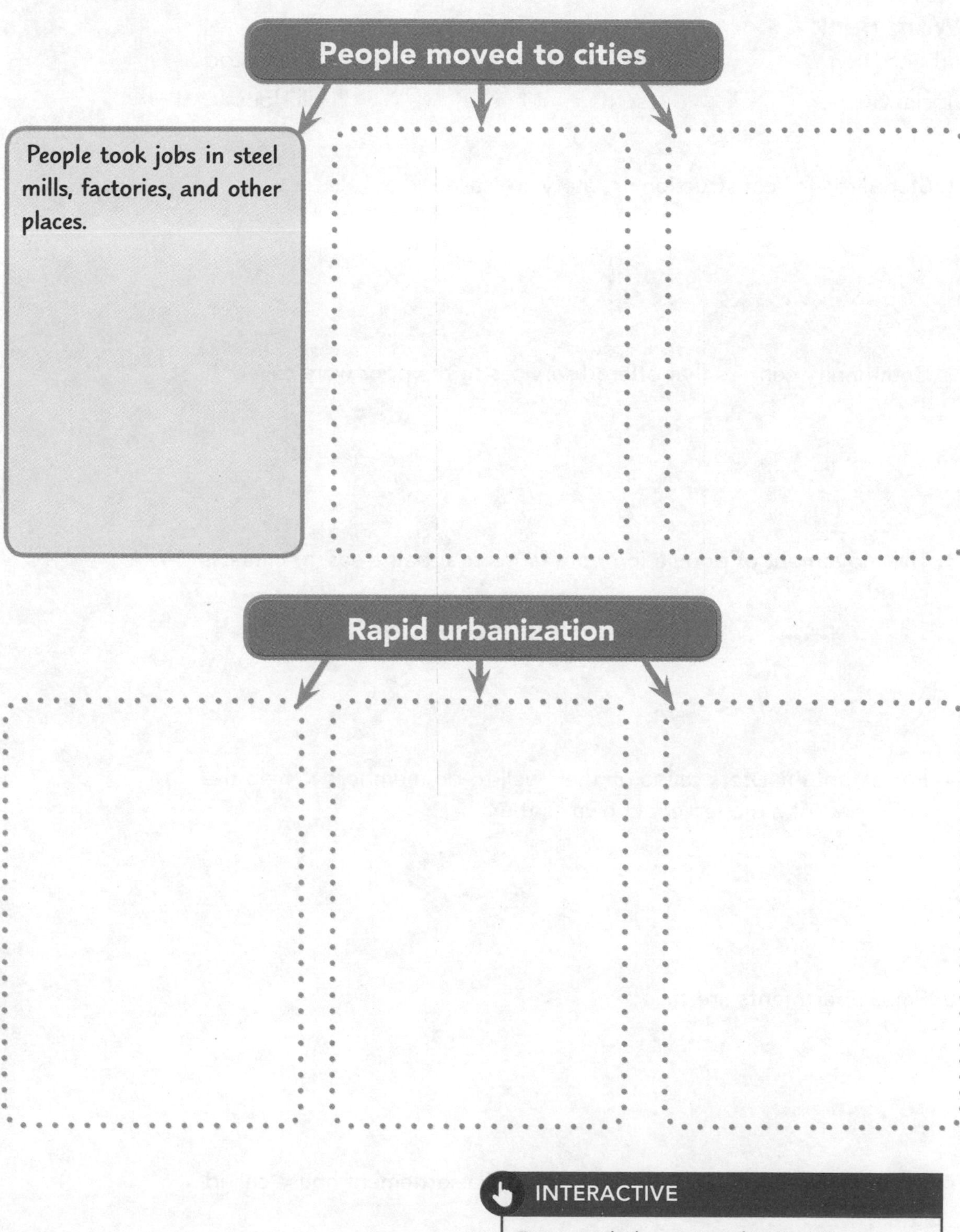
People moved to cities
People took jobs in steel mills, factories, and other places.
Rapid urbanization

INTERACTIVE

For extra help, review the 21st Century Tutorial: **Analyze Cause and Effect.**

Practice Vocabulary

Sentence Builder **Finish the sentences below with a key term from this section. You may have to change the form of the words to complete the sentences.**

Word Bank

urbanization	tenement	building code
Social Gospel	settlement house	Hull House

1. Standards for construction or safety are called

2. Community centers that offered services to the poor were called

3. The movement of population from farms to urban areas, or cities, is called

4. Protestant ministers called on their well-to-do members to help the poor, part of a movement known as the

5. Small apartments are called

6. In an old mansion, Jane Addams opened a settlement house called

Quick Activity Tracing Urbanization

At the beginning of the 1900s, many people moved to cities. Immigrants and Americans who lived in rural areas moved to cities like Boston and New York. The growth of the cities can be seen by looking at old maps. Compare these two maps of Queens, a borough of New York City, to see how urbanization changed from the first map, showing 1900, to the second map, showing 1930.

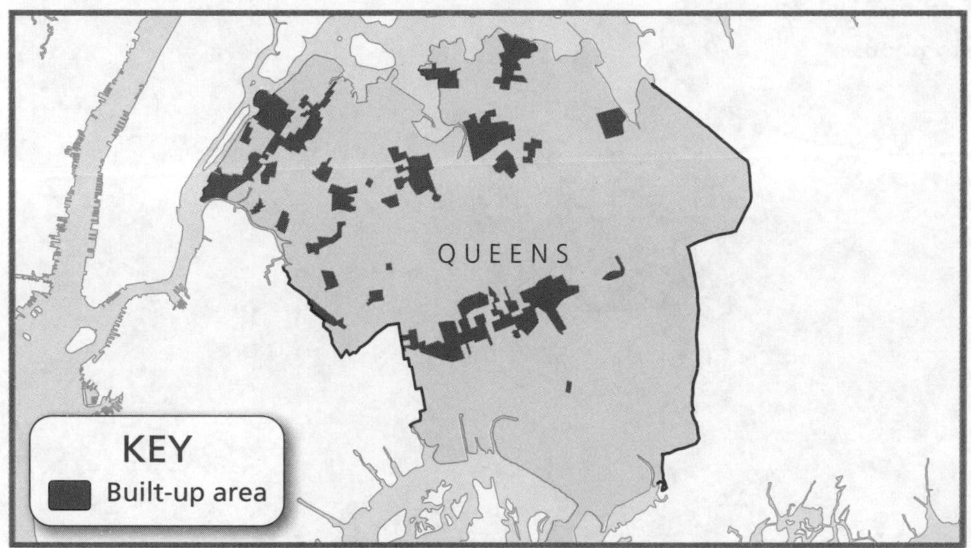

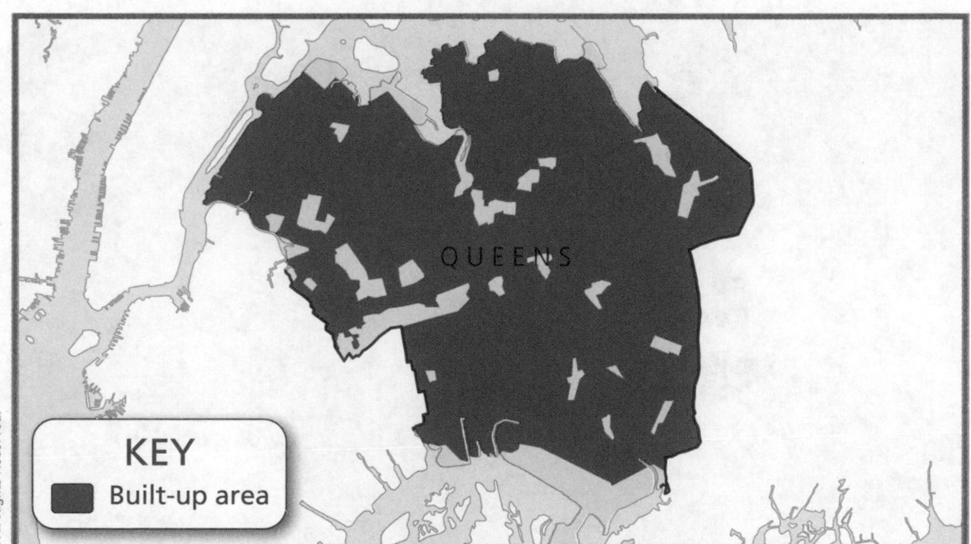

Team Challenge! **Create two maps for a fictional city, one showing the city as it looks today and another showing what the city will look like in thirty years. The future map should show that the city has grown substantially.**

Take Notes

Literacy Skills: Identify Supporting Details Use what you have read to complete the graphic organizers. In the outer circles enter details that support the main idea in the center. The first one has been partially completed for you.

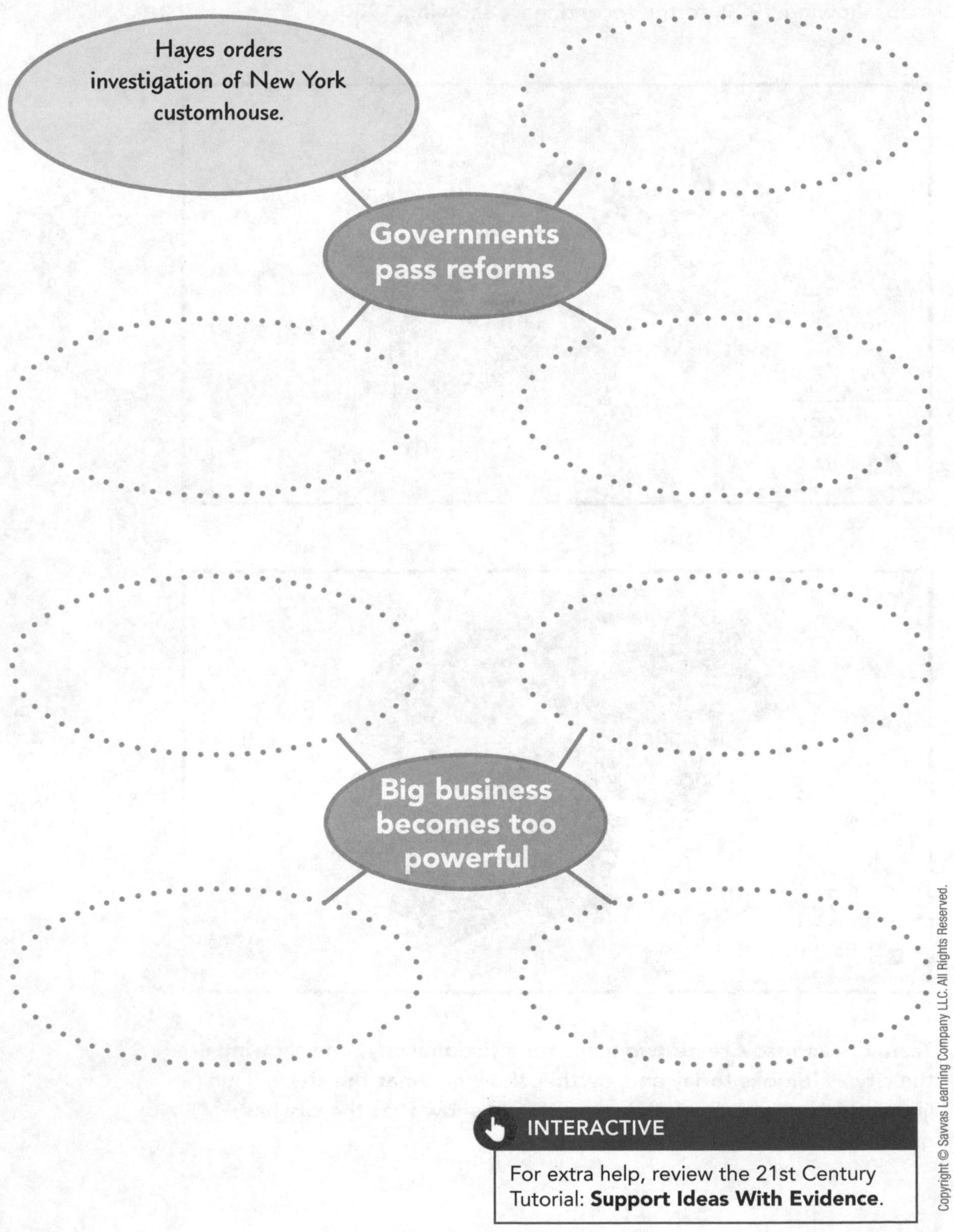

INTERACTIVE

For extra help, review the 21st Century Tutorial: **Support Ideas With Evidence**.

Practice Vocabulary

Vocabulary Quiz Show Some quiz shows ask a question and expect the contestant to give the answer. In other shows, the contestant is given an answer and must supply the question. If the blank is in the Question column, write the question that would result in the answer in the Answer column. If the question is supplied, write the answer.

Question	Answer
1.	1. Progressives
2.	2. civil service
3. What is an election in which voters choose a political party's candidate for the general election?	3.
4. What allows voters to remove an elected official from office?	4.
5.	5. muckrakers
6.	6. initiative
7. What is it called when elected officials give jobs to political supporters?	7.
8.	8. referendum

Take Notes

Literacy Skills: Classify and Categorize Use what you have read to complete the table. Write the most important Progressive reforms proposed by each President. The first one has been started for you.

Theodore Roosevelt	• *regulated and broke up bad trusts*
William Howard Taft	
Woodrow Wilson	

INTERACTIVE

For extra help, review the 21st Century Tutorial: **Categorize**.

Practice Vocabulary

True or False? Decide whether each statement below is true or false. Circle T or F, and then explain your answer. Be sure to include the underlined vocabulary word in your explanation. The first one is done for you.

1. T / F A trustbuster is a person who wants to control, or regulate, trusts.
False; Trustbusters wanted to destroy all trusts.

2. T / F The New Freedom program was designed to increase competition in the American economy.

3. T / F The Federal Reserve Act allows the government to investigate companies and order them to stop using unfair practices to destroy competitors.

4. T / F Theodore Roosevelt promised to provide a Square Deal because he believed all Americans should have the same opportunity to succeed.

5. T / F In 1912, supporters of Theodore Roosevelt became known as the Bull Moose Party because he accepted the nomination of the Progressive Party by saying, "I feel as strong as a bull moose."

6. T / F The Federal Trade Commission set up an organization that controls the supply of money to the U.S. financial system and sets interest rates.

7. T / F Theodore Roosevelt's commitment to conservation led to the creation of the National Forest Service and the creation of national parks.

Take Notes

Literacy Skills: Determine Central Ideas Use what you have read to complete the flowcharts. In the top box, write the central idea, then complete the lower boxes with missing details. Both organizers have been partially completed for you.

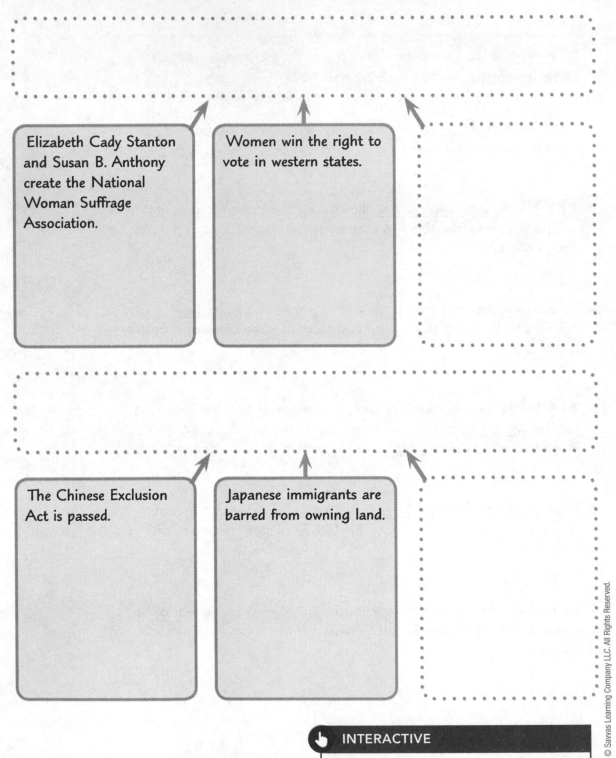

Elizabeth Cady Stanton and Susan B. Anthony create the National Woman Suffrage Association.

Women win the right to vote in western states.

The Chinese Exclusion Act is passed.

Japanese immigrants are barred from owning land.

INTERACTIVE

For extra help, review the 21st Century Tutorial: **Identify Main Ideas and Details**.

Practice Vocabulary

Matching Logic **Using your knowledge of the underlined vocabulary words, draw a line from each sentence in Column 1 to match it with the sentence in Column 2 to which it logically belongs.**

Column 1	Column 2
1. More than 1,000 African Americans were lynched in the 1890s.	In 1919, it became illegal to sell alcoholic drinks anywhere in the United States.
2. Mexican Americans and Mexican immigrants formed *mutualistas*.	Members pooled money to buy insurance and pay for legal advice.
3. Women fought very hard for many years for suffrage.	The mobs that murdered African Americans outraged people like Ida B. Wells.
4. Mexicans preserved their language and culture in barrios.	One of its founders, W.E.B. Du Bois, wanted to actively fight discrimination.
5. People in the temperance movement wanted to enact prohibition.	Elizabeth Cady Stanton and Susan B. Anthony fought in the 1800s for a constitutional amendment to give women the right to vote.
6. The National Association for the Advancement of Colored People (NAACP) worked for equal rights for African Americans.	Traditional festivals were celebrated in these neighborhoods.

Take Notes

Literacy Skills: Analyze Text Structure **Use what you have read to complete the outline, summarizing the main ideas of the lesson. The first one has been partially completed for you.**

I. Changes and Challenges in City Life
   A. Touching the Sky
      1. Skyscrapers were tall buildings with many floors.
      2. First skyscraper was built in Chicago.
      3.
   B. Transportation Innovations
      1. Electric streetcar was developed.
      2.
      3.
   C. Places to Relax
      1. Frederick Law Olmsted planned Central Park in New York City.
      2.
   D. A New Pastime
      1. Departments stores opened, with more goods at cheaper prices.
      2.

II. Why Did Sports Become Popular?
   A.
      1.
      2.
   B.
      1.
      2.
   C.
      1.
      2.

INTERACTIVE

For extra help, review the 21st Century Tutorial: **Summarize**.

Practice Vocabulary

Sentence Revision **Revise each sentence so that the underlined vocabulary word is used logically. Be sure not to change the vocabulary word. The first one is done for you.**

1. Writers who practiced yellow journalism reported stories that business and government leaders wanted to read.
   Writers who practiced yellow journalism reported stories that covered scandals, crime, and gossip.

2. Ragtime was a form of music with a slow, calming sound.

3. Architects designed skyscrapers, which are buildings with few floors that were made of wood.

4. Writers, like Mark Twain, used local color to make their stories more fantastical.

5. A suburb is a residential area in the center of the city.

6. A group of writers, called realists, depicted an idealized version of life.

7. People went to vaudeville shows to see the opera.

Writing Workshop Research Paper

Write a research paper that answers this question: **What is a significant change in American culture or society that occurred during the Progressive Era?** The prompts below will help walk you through the process.

Lesson 1 Writing Task: Generate Questions to Focus Research

(See Student Text, page 570)

In the box below, write two to four questions about a significant change in American culture or society during the Progressive Era to help focus your research.

Lesson 2 and 3 Writing Task: Find and Use Credible Sources

(See Student Text, pages 578 and 588)

Look for reliable sources. Be aware that a lot of information on the Internet is wrong or misleading. Take notes, recording information that you may use in your paper. Record Web addresses and other source information so you can return to them and cite accurately.

Source	Notes

Lesson 4 Writing Task: Support Ideas with Evidence
(See Student Text, page 596)

Outline your research paper by writing your main ideas. Next to each main idea, write facts and other evidence that support that idea.

Main Idea	Evidence

Lesson 5 Writing Task: Cite Sources (See Student Text, page 608)

Review the sources that you noted. On another piece of paper, write citations for all your sources, following the format your teacher provided. Include the name of the article or text, the author, the publisher, the date of publication, and the Web address (if applicable).

Lesson 6 Writing Task: Use Technology to Produce and Publish
(See Student Text, page 618)

When you are ready to write your paper, use available technology and share it with your classmates online.

Writing Task (See Student Text, page 621)

Using your notes, write a research paper that answers this question: What is a significant change in American culture or society that occurred during the Progressive Era? Explain why this change was so significant and how it made an impact.

Acknowledgments

Photography

002: Iberfoto/SuperStock; **018:** Archive Images/Alamy Stock Photo; **019:** Digital Image Library/Alamy Stock Photo; **022:** Vlad G/Shutterstock; **028:** Archive Images/Alamy Stock Photo; **038:** World History Archive/Alamy Stock Photo; **041:** Culture Club/ Getty Images; **042:** Albert Knapp/Alamy Stock Photo; **043:** Orhan Cam/Shutterstock; **045:** Ken Cedeno/Corbis/Getty Images; **052:** Hulton Archive/MPI/Getty Images; **061:** Cartoonist Group; **066:** North Wind Picture Archives/Alamy Stock Photo; **068:** Orhan Cam/ Shutterstock; **069:** Carol M Highsmith/Library of Congress Prints and Photographs Division Washington[LC-DIG-highsm-09904]; **070:** Science Source; **071:** GL Archive/Alamy Stock Photo; **073:** Lanmas/Alamy Stock Photo; **074:** The Metropolitan Museum of Art/ Art Resource, NY; **080:** Library of Congress Prints and Photographs Division Washington[LC-DIG-ppmsca-31832]; **092:** W H Jackson/ MPI/Getty Images; **094B:** Underwood Archives/Getty Images; **094T:** Prisma Archivo/Alamy Stock Photo; **096:** Carol M. Highsmith/Library of Congress Prints and Photographs Division[LC-DIG-highsm-27900]; **097:** World History Archive/Alamy Stock Photo; **099:** World History Archive/Alamy Stock Photo; **104:** Heritage Image Partnership Ltd/ Alamy Stock Photo; **117:** Hulton Archive/Getty Images; **120:** Niday Picture Library/Alamy Stock Photo; **122:** UIG/Underwood Archives/ Akg-images; **123:** North Wind Picture Archives/Alamy Stock Photo; **124:** Courtesy of the New York Public Library; **125:** North Wind Picture Archives/Alamy Stock Photo; **127:** Hulton Archive/Staff/ Getty Images; **128:** Picture History/Newscom; **129:** American Anti-Slavery Society/Library of Congress Rare Book and Special Collections Division Washington[LC-USZC4-5321]; **138:** Photo12/ UIG/Getty Images; **146:** John Parrot/Stocktrek Images/Alamy Stock Photo; **148:** Katherine Frey/The Washington Post/Getty Images; **149:** Everett Collection Inc/Alamy Stock Photo; **150:** Abraham Lincoln (1809–65) in public debate with Stephen A. Douglas (1813–61) in Illinois, 1858 (colour litho), American School, (19th century)/Private Collection/Peter Newark American Pictures/Bridgeman Art Library; **151:** The New York Historical Society/Contributor/Getty Images; **153:** H.Armstrong Roberts/ClassicStock/Alamy Stock Photo; **154:** Abraham Lincoln with Allan Pinkerton and Major General John A. McClernand, 1862 (b/w photo), Gardner, Alexander (1821–82)/Collection of the New-York Historical Society, USA/Bridgeman Art Library; **155:** Lawcain/Fotolia; **160:** Jerry Pinkney/National Geographic Creative/ Alamy Stock Photo; **172:** LOC Photo/Alamy Stock Photo; **175:** Charles Sumner (1811–74), US Senator; photo by George Warren, Boston (albumen print), American Photographer, (19th century)/ American Antiquarian Society, Worcester, Massachusetts, USA/ Bridgeman Art Library; **176:** Lightfoot/Getty Images; **177:** Universal Images Group North America LLC/Encyclopaedia Britannica, Inc./ Library of Congress/Alamy Stock Photo; **179:** MPI/Getty Images; **181:** Artokoloro Quint Lox Limited/Alamy Stock Photo; **194:** AKG Images; **197:** Glasshouse Images/JT Vintage/Alamy Stock Photo; **198:** Topham/The Image Works; **199:** The Stampede, 1912 (oil on canvas), Leigh, William Robinson (1866–1955)/Private Collection/ Peter Newark Western Americana/Bridgeman Art Library; **201:** Andrey Yurlov/Shutterstock; **208:** MPI/Archive Photos/Getty Images; **217B:** SSPL/Getty Images; **217T:** CSU Archives/Everett Collection/ Alamy Stock Photo; **220:** Topical Press Agency/Hulton Archive/Getty Images; **222:** Josef Hanus/Shutterstock; **223:** Library of Congress Prints and Photographs Division Washington[LC-DIG-highsm-25215]; **224:** Keystone-France/Gamma-Keystone/Getty Images; **225:** North Wind Picture Archives/Alamy Stock Photo; **228:** Photo Researchers, Inc/Alamy Stock Photo; **229:** Bettmann/Getty Images; **232B:** Sausage department at Armour and Company's meatpacking factory, Chicago, Illinois, USA. Men and boys stuffing sausage skins. Photograph c1893./Universal History Archive/UIG/Bridgeman Art Library; **232T:** FPG/Archive Photos/Getty Images;